REA's

REASONING BUILDER

for Admission & Standardized Tests

by the staff of
Research & Education Association

RESEARCH & EDUCATION ASSOCIATION
61 Ethel Road West • Piscataway, New Jersey 08854

REA's REASONING BUILDER
for Admission & Standardized Tests

Printed in the United States of America

Library of Congress Catalog Card Number 93-85671

International Standard Book Number 0-87891-932-5

Research & Education Association
61 Ethel Road West
Piscataway, NJ 08854

*REA supports the effort to conserve
and protect environmental resources
by using recycled papers.*

CONTENTS

About Research and Education Association

REA is an organization of educators, scientists, and engineers specializing in various academic fields. REA was founded in 1959 for the purpose of disseminating the most recently developed scientific information to groups in industry, government, and universities. Since then, REA has become a successful and highly respected publisher of study aids, test preps, handbooks, and reference works.

REA's Test Preparation series extensively prepares students and professionals for the Medical College Admission Test (MCAT), Graduate Record Examinations (GRE), Graduate Management Admission Test (GMAT), Advanced Placement Exams, College Board Achievement Tests/ SAT II, and the Scholastic Assessment Test (SAT I).

REA's publications and education materials are highly regarded for their significant contribution to the quest for excellence that characterizes today's educational goals. We continually receive an unprecedented amount of praise from professional instructors, librarians, parents, and students for our published books. Our authors are as diverse as the subjects and fields represented in the books we publish. They are well-known in their respective fields and serve on the faculties of prestigious universities throughout the United States.

Acknowledgments

Special recognition is extended to the following persons:

Dr. Max Fogiel, President, for his overall guidance which has brought this publication to completion.

Stacey A. Sporer, Managing Editor, for directing the editorial staff throughout each phase of the project.

Lori Glickman, Project Editor, for coordinating the development of the book.

Theodora Glitsky, M.A. and Wesley G. Phelan, Ph.D. for their significant contributions.

Joanne Morbit, Typesetter, for typesetting the book.

CHAPTER 1

About the Reasoning Builder

About This Book

REA's staff of authors and educators have prepared material, exercises, and tests based on each of the major standardized exams, including the GRE, GMAT, LSAT, SAT, PSAT, ACT, NTE, MCAT, CBEST, PPST, and other teacher certification tests. The types of questions represented on these standardized exams have been analyzed in order to produce the most comprehensive preparatory material possible. You will find review material, helpful strategies, and exercises geared to your level of studying.

How To Use This Book

If you are preparing to take the GRE, GMAT, or LSAT, you will be taking a test requiring excellent logical and analytical reasoning ability. This book comprises a comprehensive logical and analytical review which can be tailored to your specific test preparation needs.

Locate your test on the chart below and find the corresponding section(s) recommended for study. REA suggests that you study the indicated material thoroughly as a review for your test.

	Logical/Critical Reasoning Chapter 3 Pages 35-74	Analytical Reasoning Chapter 6 Pages 123-204
GMAT	X	
GRE	X	X
LSAT	X	X

This book will help you prepare for your test since it includes different types of questions and drills that are representative of your specific test. The book also includes diagnostic tests so that you can determine your strengths and weaknesses within each subject. The explanations are clear and comprehensive, and not only explain why the answer is correct, but also why the remaining answers are incorrect. This book will give you practice within a wide range of categories and question types.

The Logical/Critical Reasoning Chapter will prepare students for questions on the GMAT, GRE, and LSAT which involve drawing conclusions from a set of given conditions as well as identifying and recognizing various arguments and the assumptions which can be made from them.

The Analytical Reasoning Chapter will provide practice with questions that involve deducing new information from a given set of related statements. Although these questions do not require knowledge of formal logic or mathematics, they do require knowledge of vocabulary and simple computational ability.

Finally, before you get started, here are a few guidelines:

➤ Study full chapters. If you think after a few minutes that the chapter appears easy, continue studying. Many chapters (like the tests themselves) become more difficult as they continue.

➤ Use this guide as a supplement to the review materials provided by the test administrators.

As you prepare for a standardized test, you will want to review some of the basic concepts and formats of various reasoning questions. The more familiar you are with the fundamental principles, the better you will do on your test. Our reviews represent the types of questions and topics that appear on the reasoning portions of standardized tests.

Most of the concepts presented on the test are ones with which you are already familiar. Simply review them in order to score well.

Along with knowledge of the question types, how quickly and accurately you answer reasoning questions will have an effect on your success. All tests have time limits, so the more questions you can answer correctly in the given period of time, the better off you will be. Our suggestion is that you make sure to complete the drills as you review and take the practice test when you feel confident with the material. Pay special attention to both the time it takes to complete the test and the number of correct answers.

CHAPTER 2

Logical and Critical Reasoning Diagnostic Test

LOGICAL AND CRITICAL REASONING DIAGNOSTIC TEST

1. Ⓐ Ⓑ Ⓒ Ⓓ Ⓔ
2. Ⓐ Ⓑ Ⓒ Ⓓ Ⓔ
3. Ⓐ Ⓑ Ⓒ Ⓓ Ⓔ
4. Ⓐ Ⓑ Ⓒ Ⓓ Ⓔ
5. Ⓐ Ⓑ Ⓒ Ⓓ Ⓔ
6. Ⓐ Ⓑ Ⓒ Ⓓ Ⓔ
7. Ⓐ Ⓑ Ⓒ Ⓓ Ⓔ
8. Ⓐ Ⓑ Ⓒ Ⓓ Ⓔ
9. Ⓐ Ⓑ Ⓒ Ⓓ Ⓔ
10. Ⓐ Ⓑ Ⓒ Ⓓ Ⓔ
11. Ⓐ Ⓑ Ⓒ Ⓓ Ⓔ
12. Ⓐ Ⓑ Ⓒ Ⓓ Ⓔ
13. Ⓐ Ⓑ Ⓒ Ⓓ Ⓔ
14. Ⓐ Ⓑ Ⓒ Ⓓ Ⓔ
15. Ⓐ Ⓑ Ⓒ Ⓓ Ⓔ
16. Ⓐ Ⓑ Ⓒ Ⓓ Ⓔ
17. Ⓐ Ⓑ Ⓒ Ⓓ Ⓔ
18. Ⓐ Ⓑ Ⓒ Ⓓ Ⓔ
19. Ⓐ Ⓑ Ⓒ Ⓓ Ⓔ
20. Ⓐ Ⓑ Ⓒ Ⓓ Ⓔ
21. Ⓐ Ⓑ Ⓒ Ⓓ Ⓔ
22. Ⓐ Ⓑ Ⓒ Ⓓ Ⓔ
23. Ⓐ Ⓑ Ⓒ Ⓓ Ⓔ
24. Ⓐ Ⓑ Ⓒ Ⓓ Ⓔ
25. Ⓐ Ⓑ Ⓒ Ⓓ Ⓔ
26. Ⓐ Ⓑ Ⓒ Ⓓ Ⓔ
27. Ⓐ Ⓑ Ⓒ Ⓓ Ⓔ
28. Ⓐ Ⓑ Ⓒ Ⓓ Ⓔ
29. Ⓐ Ⓑ Ⓒ Ⓓ Ⓔ
30. Ⓐ Ⓑ Ⓒ Ⓓ Ⓔ

Logical and Critical Reasoning
Diagnostic Test

This diagnostic test is designed to help you determine your strengths and your weaknesses in logical and critical reasoning. The diagnostic test is set up in the same format that appears on many standardized tests. It contains all of the various question types which you are likely to encounter while taking these exams. By taking this diagnostic test, you will be able to determine which question types pose the most difficulty for you. It is wise to study all the material contained within the reviews, but by taking this diagnostic test, you will be able to determine the areas in which you are the weakest, and concentrate on those particular question types.

These types of questions are found on the following tests: GMAT, GRE, and LSAT

Diagnostic Test

DIRECTIONS: The questions in this section are based on the reasoning contained in brief statements or passages. For some questions, more than one of the choices could conceivably answer the question. However, you are to choose the **best** answer; that is, the response that most accurately and completely answers the question. You should not make assumptions that are by common-sense standards implausible, superfluous, or incompatible with the passage.

---

1. The town of Modern, USA, drinks Fizzy Pop after a hot day in the sun. Buy yours today!

    A reader who is not a resident of Modern, USA, would be most likely to purchase Fizzy Pop if he or she drew which of the following questionable conclusions invited by the advertisement?

    (A) Among many thirst quenchers, Fizzy Pop is the best after a day in the sun.

    (B) Many modern people use Fizzy Pop to quench their thirst; I should get on that bandwagon!

    (C) An entire town cannot be wrong; the numbers prove it.

    (D) Famous people in Modern use Fizzy; I should, too.

    (E) The advertisement is placed where those who have much leisure time can read it.

Questions 2 and 3 are based on the following.

The defeated candidate addressed her political party tonight at the final gathering of this election year. She talked to them about the platform of her opponent and pointed out many questions he left unanswered in their recent televised debate. She concluded by listing the many defeats suffered by Abraham Lincoln before he finally was elected President of the United States. She stated that she planned to pursue her political career despite this defeat.

2. The method of gaining support used by the defeated candidate was to

    (A) attack the character of the opponent by suggesting he equivocated by not answering questions.

    (B) imply an analogy between her experiences and those of Abraham Lincoln.

    (C) point out that the opponent's claims imply a dilemma.

    (D) show that the opponent's unanswered questions reflect an absurd lack of preparation and knowledge.

    (E) show that the platform of her opponent was absurd.

3. The defeated candidate could effectively defend her platform against the newly elected candidate by pointing out that

   (A) her expertise in answering the questions he avoided is outstanding.

   (B) she is neither inept nor immoral.

   (C) he avoided the truth in answering the questions asked.

   (D) the defeats of Abraham Lincoln were caused by similar concerns and actions.

   (E) point out that the opponent's platform leads to an absurd conclusion.

4. In 1987 the annual interest rate on new homes was 10%. In 1980 the rate was 14%. Inflation was 12% in 1980 and 4% in 1987.

   Consider the case of a person who borrows $100 for one year at 10%; she pays back the $100 plus $10 and sees the purchasing power of the debt decline by $4 due to inflation. The net payment in purchasing-power terms would be $6 or 6%.

   Which of the following corrections of a figure appearing in the passage above, if it were the only correction that needed to be made, would yield a new calculation showing that it would actually be cheaper to borrow in 1987 than in 1980?

   (A) The interest rate in 1987 was actually 8%, not 10% as previously stated.

   (B) The inflation rate in 1987 was only 2%, not 4% as previously stated.

   (C) The interest rate in 1980 was 14% with only a 4% inflation rate.

   (D) The interest rate in 1980 was 14% with a 13% inflation rate.

   (E) The interest rate in 1987 was 5%.

5.   Carl: The South has made significant progress in reducing infant deaths since 1984. Nearly all Southern states reduced their infant mortality rate between 1983 and 1987. The statistics are very encouraging.

Richard: We need to wait until all the facts are in to be encouraged. The 1987 figures do not reflect the recent facts on infant deaths due to AIDS and drug abuse. Before we take heart, we need to remember that the USA has one of the worst infant death rates of any industrialized country in the world.

Which of the following best describes the weak point in Carl's claim on which Richard's response focuses?

(A)   The evidence Carl cites comes from only a single area of the United States, the South.

(B)   The decrease may be a mathematical error.

(C)   The 1987 statistics quoted are not current enough to reflect recent occurrences.

(D)   No mention is made of Northern states in the report.

(E)   No exact figures are given for infant morality in 1984 through 1987.

Questions 6 and 7 refer to the following paragraph.

Partly in response to consumer demand and partly to compete with foreign imports, car manufacturers produced more cars during the past two years than ever before. This production resulted in less steel being available for refrigerator manufacturing. So while the volume of car production has been increasing over the two-year period, the volume of refrigerator production decreased.

6.   Which of the following can be inferred from the paragraph?

(A)   Refrigerators are a profitable product only if they are produced on a large scale.

(B)   Production of refrigerators has been unusually high for the two-year period.

(C)   Steel production will increase in the future.

(D) Surplus stocks of refrigerators have been reduced in the two-year period.

(E) The profits that car manufacturers have made are unprecedented.

7. Which of the following conclusions is warranted from the previous paragraph?

(A) Refrigerator manufacturers foresaw how high the price of refrigerators would go.

(B) Car manufacturers made more profit in the two-year period than they ever have or will again.

(C) Steel manufacturers preferred selling to refrigerator manufacturers rather than to car manufacturers even though the amount of steel might have been the same.

(D) The price of refrigerators has increased over the two-year period.

(E) The price of refrigerators has declined over the two-year period since there was no steel used in their production.

8. Researchers in Florida, Texas, and Hawaii believe they are getting closer to the day when the oil substitute hydrogen is as common as gasoline. Hydrogen will not pollute. It is one of the most abundant elements in the earth. The cost to consumers would eventually be reasonable, but now the cost is prohibitive. Skeptics prefer to keep gasoline as the major fuel for our vehicles.

Which of the following, if true, would tend to weaken the force of the skeptics' arguments?

(A) The threat of the greenhouse effect and acid rain from pollution is increasing.

(B) Hydrogen has never been used as an energy source.

(C) Future supplies of oil are guaranteed.

(D) A concerted national effort is needed.

(E) A gradual transition from gasoline to hydrogen is needed.

Questions 9 and 10 are based on the following.

When Mt. Vesuvius erupted in A.D. 79 and destroyed Pompeii, it also destroyed Herculaneum; scholars assumed the population of Herculaneum escaped to safety.

9. Which of the following pieces of evidence best refutes the hypotheses of archaeologists?

    (A) A well-digger broke through to the town in 1709.

    (B) By 1980 ten skeletons had been found.

    (C) Homes and buildings indicate more than 4,000 people lived there.

    (D) In 1982, over a five-week period, 26 complete skeletons were discovered in chambers beneath the terraces and on the beach.

    (E) The Roman beach lies 500 yards from the bay.

10. The force of the opinion of the scholars is most seriously weakened if which of the following is true?

    (A) Most of the skeletons carried their possessions with them.

    (B) Pompeii was entombed by the same eruption.

    (C) It took no more than five minutes for the hot mixture of ash, gas, and rock to reach Herculaneum.

    (D) As more digging proceeds in Herculaneum, even more skeletons will be uncovered.

    (E) The skeletons were actually located in a cemetery; the possessions were included as part of a burial rite.

11. While Governor Jencsik was in office the state's budget has increased by an average of 8% each year. While the previous governor was in office, the state's budget increased by an average of 12% each year. Obviously the budgets planned during Governor Jencsik's term have caused the intense growth in state spending.

    Which of the following would most seriously weaken the conclusion?

    (A) The rate of inflation in the state averaged 9% during the term of the previous governor and 2% each year during Jencsik's term.

(B) The rate of inflation in the state averaged 8% per year during the previous governor's term in office and 2% each year during Jencsik's term.

(C) In each year of Jencsik's office, the state's budget has shown some increase in spending over the previous year.

(D) During Jencsik's term in office, private citizens began to pay for numerous services that the state had previously paid for.

(E) During the previous governor's term in office, the state introduced several "budget austerity" packages.

12. Doctors in a recent survey recommended Swabby Cotton Swabs over Nifty Rayon Swabs. Try them today.

A reader is likely to purchase the cotton swabs if he or she drew which of the following questionable conclusions invited by the advertisement?

(A) Among swabs, cotton is better than nylon.

(B) I should join the bandwagon and use Swabbies like most Americans.

(C) The advertisement is placed where those with a high degree of education and status will be likely to read it.

(D) The doctors mentioned were helped to become professionals by their using Swabbies.

(E) If professional physicians use Swabbies, I should do so also.

13. Rosedale has a population of 40,000 people. The median family income in this town is $56,000 per year. The Chamber of Commerce has announced that a family with this median income can afford to buy a home in the $140,000 price range. This calculation was based on a 11.2% mortgage interest rate and upon the assumption that a family could afford to pay only 25% of its income for a home.

Which of the following corrections of a figure appearing in the passage above, if it were the only correction that needed to be made, would yield a new calculation showing that even incomes below the median family income would enable Rosedale families to afford the $140,000 home?

(A) Rosedale's population is 20,000.

(B) Rosedale's median family income is $28,000.

(C) Rosedale's median priced home costs $180,000.

(D) The rate at which people in Rosedale had to pay interest is only 11%.

(E) Families in Rosedale could afford to pay up to 32% of their annual income for housing.

14. Some scientists have argued that the effect of dust storms on the surface temperature of the planet Mars reliably predicts a "nuclear winter" on Earth following a nuclear war that would stir up a comparable amount of debris.

Which of the following, it true, would tend most to weaken the argument predicting a "nuclear winter"?

(A) A nuclear war is unlikely because both sides would suffer almost total annihilation.

(B) The chances of a nuclear war occurring are likely to decrease as a result of disarmament.

(C) If people understand the dangers posed by nuclear war and if people prepare adequately for a nuclear war, then they can survive it.

(D) There is no evidence of life on Mars.

(E) There is no water in the atmosphere on Mars, and therefore the effect of dust on surface temperature is not comparable to the corresponding effect on Earth.

15. The mayor of Jonesville opposes any increase this year in the salaries of police officers, pointing out that these salaries have increased 10% over the last five year.

Which of the following, if true, would most seriously weaken the mayor's argument?

(A) The rate of inflation during this five-year period was 3% annually.

(B) The salaries of the police officers are the same as the salaries of the fire fighters.

(C) The city budget shows a predicted surplus that would be more than enough to pay for a substantial increase in the salaries of police officers.

(D) A survey of public opinion shows that crime is the number one concern of the citizens of Jonesville.

(E) The mayor was accused of political corruption and nepotism in the recent election.

16. Juarez is older than Korrie.

    Lorenzo is older than Martin.

    Martin is younger then Nedino.

    Korrie and Nedino are twins.

    If the information above is true, which of the following must also be true?

    (A) Lorenzo is older than Nedino.

    (B) Lorenzo is older than Juarez.

    (C) Korrie is younger than Lorenzo.

    (D) Juarez is older than Martin.

    (E) Korrie is younger than Martin.

17. Institutional policies should be designed to help everyone associated with the institution. Groups within an institution, however, often favor policies that are helpful to them alone without taking into consideration the possibility that such policies may hurt another group within the institution. The administration of a hospital, university, or government must seek to balance these conflicting interests.

    Which of the following statements provides support for the claim above?

    I.   An increase in faculty salaries resulted in an increase in tuition.

    II. A decrease in hospital fees resulted in a decrease in wages paid to the nursing staff.

    III. Additional appointments to the fund-raising staff resulted in an increase in money available for scholarships.

    (A) I and III only.

(B) II only.

(C) I and II only.

(D) II and III only.

(E) I, II, and III.

18. Demographic studies indicate the number of elderly is increasing, and that therefore the total cost of caring for the elderly is also increasing. At the same time, the number of wage earners is not increasing as rapidly. The funds to care for the elderly will have to come from taxes paid by the wage earners.

Which of the following inferences can properly be drawn from the statements above?

(A) Unless average income increases sufficiently, the percentage of each person's income that must go to caring for the elderly will increase.

(B) The elderly will not receive adequate care.

(C) Only the rich will be able to afford care in their later years.

(D) Younger people will vote against the increase in taxes needed to care for the growing numbers of elderly.

(E) Citizens should save their own money now to take care of their own needs during retirement themselves, instead of depending on younger people to take care of them.

19. Opponents of a sales tax argue that it is a regressive tax: a flat tax of, let us say, 5% across the board might be, as a percentage of income, close to or at 5% for a poor person, but will usually be, relative to income, much lower than that for a rich person.

If the example in the statement above is accurate, which of the following can be most reliably inferred from it?

(A) Rich people pay more taxes than poor people.

(B) Most of the money collected as taxes is taken from the incomes of poor people.

(C) Rich people can afford to pay high-priced accountants to find ways for them to avoid paying taxes.

(D)   Poor people spend a larger percentage of their income than rich people.

(E)   Rich people should pay higher taxes because they can afford to.

20.   While the previous governor was in office, the state's budget increased by an average of 12%. During Governor Taylor's term of office, the state's budget increased by an average of 6% per year. Despite Governor Taylor's political promise to control state spending, his actions seem to prove otherwise.

Which of the following would most seriously support the conclusion?

(A)   The rate of inflation in the state averaged 10% during the previous governor's term in office and 4% during Taylor's term.

(B)   The rate of inflation in the state averaged 9% during the previous governor's term in office and 1% each year during Taylor's term.

(C)   In each year of Taylor's term in office, the state's budget has shown some increase in spending over the previous year.

(D)   During Taylor's term in office that state has ceased to pay for numerous services that private citizens were previously entitled to through state financing.

(E)   During the previous governor's term in office, the state introduced several so-called "austerity" measures.

Questions 21 and 22 are based on the following.

Seven former prison inmates testified at the town meeting at the request of town officials. The seven stated that the physical facilities at the local incarceration center were substandard; four presented evidence that the accommodations were so bad that their health was endangered. The former inmates suggested that unless something were done soon, a riot such as the one in the neighboring county might result. If better facilities are to be provided, however, taxes may have to be increased. Several local citizens stated that they are concerned about increasing their tax rate solely on the word of convicted felons.

21.   The method of attacking the charges of former inmates is to

(A)   attack the character of the opponents rather than their claim.

(B)   imply an analogy between their demands and the riots in another country.

(C)   point out that the inmates' claims imply a dilemma.

(D)   show that the inmates' claims lead to an absurd conclusion.

(E)   show that the prisoners' demands in a neighboring county were not met before the riot.

22.   The former inmates could effectively defend their position against the townspeople's strategy by pointing out that

(A)   the expertise of those suggesting reform is outstanding.

(B)   they are neither inept or immoral.

(C)   the practical renovation will not require a tax increase.

(D)   the riots in the next county were caused by similar concerns and actions.

(E)   the fact that riots were caused by similar concerns in one place does not mean that they would necessarily result in this instance.

23.   Good Health is the nutritional supplement preferred by the 400 accomplished or professional athletes who subscribe to this paper, the *Health Bulletin*. Shouldn't you give their preferred supplement a try?

A reader who is not a professional athlete would be most likely to purchase the nutritional supplement if he or she drew which of the following questionable conclusions invited by the advertisement?

(A)   Among nutritional supplements, Good Health is the most nutritionally complete.

(B)   Professional athletes cannot do their jobs properly without taking Good Health.

(C)   The advertisement is placed where those who will be likely to read it are accomplished or professional athletes.

(D)   The athletes mentioned were helped to become accomplished or professional athletes by using Good Health.

(E)   Only those who will in fact become accomplished or professional will read the advertisement.

Questions 24 and 25 are based on the following.

In July 1984 Richard Leakey and colleague Kamoya Kimeu found in Nairobi an almost entire *Homo erectus* skeleton, the first recovered that was 1.6 million years old. The skeleton was that of a boy about 12 years of age. He was about five feet four inches tall and probably would have reached a height of six feet. His bones had been scattered and trampled in a swamp. In parts and proportion they were much like the human form today. Under him was volcanic material dating from 1.65 million years ago.

24. Which of the following hypotheses is best supported by the evidence above?

    (A) This spectacular find confirms that the human form as we know it today only recently developed.

    (B) The remains may have confused two different time periods.

    (C) The body may not be as old as believed because it could have fallen through a large burrow dug by a gerbil in the area.

    (D) The body could have been imported to the area by a religious group which used human sacrifices.

    (E) This find confirms the antiquity of the human form.

25. The evidence from the find most seriously supports which of the following?

    (A) The belief that humans did not exist 1.6 million years ago.

    (B) The belief that people did not look like humans until 100 B.C.

    (C) The belief that humans reached their present size more than a million and a half years ago, with some populations in poor areas becoming smaller recently.

    (D) The belief that humans have grown larger through time.

    (E) The belief that human life really began on the continent of Europe.

26. Psychologists continue to debate the issue of whether people have a dominant side of their brain which controls reasoning and actions or whether both sides of the brain work together. Proponents of the split-brain theory suggest that a right-brained person is creative, intuitive since this individual uses the right hemisphere. On the other hand, they contend that the left-brained individual uses the verbal, language-oriented, logical hemisphere of the brain to control most of their actions/thinking.

Which of the following, if true, would strengthen the position of the opponents to the split-brain theory?

(A) When surgery is performed to disconnect the two sides of the brain, both sides continue to operate well — but not perfectly.

(B) When a patient has right hemisphere damage, no logical disorders are manifested.

(C) Because of the independent functions of the two hemispheres, an activity might engage one hemisphere of the brain and not another.

(D) The hemispheres operate independently because of specialized functions.

(E) It is impossible to educate one side of the brain without educating the other.

Questions 27 and 28 are based on the following.

In 1985 eight mummified bodies originally found in the 1970's in Greenland were subjected to careful analysis. The bodies — five in one place, three in another — were found in chambers in the rocks. The bodies were so well-preserved that at first the six-month-old infant was believed to be a doll. The bodies were placed in the chamber about 1475.

27. Which of the following reasons for the bodies being in the caves is best supported by the evidence presented above?

(A) The people drowned and the bodies washed into the crevices near the sea.

(B) The people died of starvation in the small caves.

(C) The people died from smallpox.

(D)   The people had huddled there and had frozen to death.

(E)   The bodies of the dead had probably been placed there by family members.

28.   Which of the following theories best explains why the bodies were preserved so well without embalming?

(A)   The hot, dry air of Greenland preserved the bodies.

(B)   Dehydrating winds and low temperatures preserved the bodies.

(C)   The bodies had only recently been placed there.

(D)   The moisture near the shore preserved the bodies.

(E)   Lightning striking the area preserved the corpses.

29.   Alvin is trying to choose between an inexpensive, two-door subcompact and a roomier, more stylish car that costs several thousand dollars more. He is probably going to buy the subcompact. It gets much better mileage, and there has been a recent increase in the cost of gasoline. Given Alvin's present salary, after taxes and living expenses, he can budget about $300 for car payments. The finance company is offering Alvin a five-year loan at 5% with $1,000 down. At that rate he would not be able to make the payments on the more expensive car. In addition, Alvin must consider insurance. He could reduce the premiums by opting for a policy with high deductibles, but after making the downpayment he would not have enough money in his savings account to cover the deductibles in case of an accident.

Which of the following changes would make it easier for Alvin to afford the more expensive car?

(A)   The state increases the amount of liability insurance every car owner is required to carry.

(B)   Alvin chooses the insurance policy with the lowest deductibles.

(C)   Alvin chooses to pay the lowest possible downpayment.

(D)   The finance company lowers the interest rate on Alvin's car loan.

(E)   The mileage claimed for the cars by the manufacturer is higher than the actual mileage Alvin will get driving to work.

30. Food stamp figures are a means of gauging economic well-being. A decline in food stamps issued indicates a healthy economy.

Which of the following statements refutes most completely the author's claim that a decrease in issued food stamps indicates a healthy economy?

(A) Three years ago a robust economy accompanied a decline in food stamps issued.

(B) Food stamps are funded by the federal government.

(C) Population figures continue to rise while food stamps issued decreased.

(D) The application process has recently become more strict which has made it necessary for "food kitchens" to help with many who would have previously received food stamps.

(E) All deserving people currently receive food stamps.

LOGICAL AND CRITICAL REASONING DIAGNOSTIC TEST

1. (B)	7. (D)	13. (E)	19. (D)	25. (C)
2. (B)	8. (A)	14. (E)	20. (B)	26. (E)
3. (A)	9. (D)	15. (A)	21. (A)	27. (E)
4. (E)	10. (D)	16. (D)	22. (A)	28. (B)
5. (C)	11. (D)	17. (C)	23. (D)	29. (D)
6. (D)	12. (E)	18. (A)	24. (E)	30. (D)

Logical and Critical Reasoning
Diagnostic Test
Detailed Explanations OF Answers

1.   **(B)**   The advertisement does not suggest any comparison between Fizzy Pop and other thirst quenchers; (A) is not the best choice. (B) is the correct answer; the suggestion here is that a lot of "modern" residents use Fizzy Pop. People often want to follow the crowd and get on the bandwagon. This advertisement appeals to those individuals. (C) is a possibility, but it is certainly not the best choice. Numbers are only suggested in this ad. There are no numbers stated for the individual to use. (D) is not the correct choice since no famous people are alluded to in this advertisement. (E) is not the best choice because no indication is given as to where the advertisement appeared.

2.   **(B)**   There is no direct evidence to suggest that the defeated candidate attacked the character of the elected individual; therefore, (A) is not the appropriate choice. The candidate did make a comparison between her defeat and those of Lincoln; (B) is the correct answer. Little information is given about the opponent's claims so (C) is not the best choice. The reader is not given the reason for pointing out the unanswered questions. Perhaps he did not have the knowledge. Perhaps he was dishonest and avoided them. Perhaps he did not respond to the wishes of the people he is to serve. (D) is a possible choice, but it is not the best choice since there are so many unanswered questions about it. According to the passage, the defeated candidate did not directly show that the opponent's platform was absurd; hence, (E) is not the best choice.

3.   **(A)**   (A) is the best choice. Since the opponent failed to answer certain questions, she could demonstrate her expertise by answering the questions. The defeated candidate did not, according to the passage, make direct reference to her morality or capabilities; therefore, (B) is incorrect. Again, the truth may not have been avoided in the failure to answer questions by the opponent; (C) is not the correct choice. The concerns and actions which brought about Lincoln's defeats seem irrelevant at this point, so (D) is incorrect. It seems too late now to discuss the absurd conclusion to which the opponent's platform may lead. The passage does not even indicate that such is the case; therefore, (E) is not the best choice.

4. **(E)** (A) is not the best choice. If the inflation rate in 1987 remained 4% and the interest rate was 8% (rather than 10%), the cost for borrowing would actually be 4%—down from the 6% originally calculated. This would not be below the 2% sought. If the inflation rate in 1987 was 2% — not 4% — and the interest rate remains 10%, the cost would be 8%. This is above the 2% calculated for 1980; therefore, (B) is not the best choice. If the interest rate in 1980 was 14% with a 4% inflation rate, this would yield a cost of 10%. This is above the 1987 cost, so (C) is incorrect. If the interest rate in 1980 was 14% with a 13% inflation rate, the cost of borrowing would be 1%; the cost in 1987 would still exceed this, thus (D) would not be the best choice. If the interest rate in 1987 was 5% and the inflation rate were 4%, the cost of borrowing money would be 1% — less than the cost in 1980; hence, (E) is the correct answer.

5. **(C)** It is true that Carl is citing only a single area of the United States, but that was his explicit purpose. This is not the weak point that Richard is concerned about, thus (A) is incorrect. There is no indication made that the decrease is a mathematical error; (B) is not the correct answer. The fact that the 1987 statistics are not current enough to reflect recent occurrences is the weak point that Richard responds to at once; therefore, (C) is the best choice. Richard does not focus on the fact that Carl makes no mention of Northern states; (D) is not the best choice. Richard does not ask for exact figures for infant mortality for 1984 — 1987. He seems to be more concerned with the lack of current information, so (E) is not the correct answer.

6. **(D)** Refrigerators can be a profitable product when they are produced on a small scale if the demand is there; (A) is incorrect. The passage states that the production of refrigerators has been unusually low for the two-year period since the steel has gone to automobiles; therefore, (B) is incorrect. (C) is not the best choice, since the passage does not speculate on whether steel production will increase in the future. (D) is the best answer; with the decrease in refrigerator production, the surplus stocks of refrigerators have been decreased. (E) is not the best choice since the passage does not suggest whether the profits of car manufacturers are unprecedented.

7. **(D)** It would have been impossible for refrigerator manufacturers to foresee how high the price of refrigerators would actually go; therefore, (A) is not the best choice. (B) cannot be ascertained from the passage. Just what the profit margin was for cars in the past or what it will be in the future was not discussed. Since there is no evidence in the passage to suggest that steel manufacturers would prefer selling to either the car or refrigerator producers (in some instances they may be one and the same), (C) is not the best choice. The price of

refrigerators has increased since supply was down and demand was there; (D) is the best choice. There is no evidence in the passage to suggest a less expensive substance was substituted for steel in refrigerators, which eliminates (E).

8.   **(A)**   The greenhouse effect and acid rain are both consequences of environmental pollution, much of which can be attributed to gasoline being used for vehicles. This threat to the environment could certainly be helped with the use of hydrogen fuel. Using hydrogen to help eliminate pollution would weaken arguments skeptics might have; (A) is the best choice. (B) should not be selected since hydrogen has been used as an energy source for rockets. Since future supplies of oil are *not* guaranteed, (C) is not the best choice. (D) is not the best answer. A concerted national effort is needed to utilize hydrogen as a fuel, but this is not an argument which would weaken the arguments of the skeptics. Certainly a gradual transition from gasoline to hydrogen is needed, but this does not serve to weaken the skeptics' arguments; (E) is not the best choice.

9.   **(D)**   (A) is not the best choice; the fact that a well-digger broke through to the town in 1709 does not refute the opinion of the scholars. Finding only ten skeletons would not refute the opinion of the scholars; (B) should not be selected. Empty homes and buildings, again, would not refute the opinion of the scholars; (C) should not be chosen. Finding 26 skeletons in such a short period of time would be the best choice upon which to base the opposition to the theory of the scholars. Thus, (D) is the best choice. The fact that it was so far to the bay from the beach may have made it more difficult for the people to escape, but it is not sufficient evidence upon which to base the opposition to the theory of the scholars; (E) should not be selected as the best answer.

10.   **(D)**   The fact that most skeletons had possessions with them is not sufficient to weaken the force of the opinion of the scholars. The possessions could have been included as part of a burial rite; (A) should not be chosen. The fact that Pompeii was entombed by the same eruption does not weaken the force of the scholars substantially; (B) is not the best choice. The speed with which the molten mass reached the city could weaken the force of the opinion of the scholars, but it is not the best choice; (C) should not be selected. The scholars' opinion is most weakened if even more skeletons in a supposed state of flight when they were buried are uncovered; therefore, (D) would be the best choice. Finding the skeletons in a cemetery with possessions included as part of a burial rite would not weaken the opinion; (E) is not the best choice.

11. **(D)** The previous governor's spending averaged 12% but the inflation rate was 9%; this means the cost was 3%. Governor Jencsik's spending was 8%, but the rate of inflation was 2%; this means the cost was 6%, 3% higher than during the previous administration. This shows that the rate of spending increased. Since the reader is looking for a statement that would weaken the conclusion that Governor Jencsik's budgets have caused intense growth in state spending, (A) is not the proper answer, it actually strengthens the argument. During the previous governor's term, the increase was 12% minus 8%, or a total of 4%. During Jencsik's term the increase was 8% with an inflation rate of 2%, for a 6% increase. Since Jencsik's rate of state spending was above that of the previous governor, this supports the conclusion that there was growth in state spending. Since the reader is asked to look for an answer which would weaken the conclusion, (B) is not the right answer. Again, (C) seems to support, not weaken, the conclusion that Jencsik's budgets increased state spending. If citizens are assuming responsibility for services that the state normally paid, then (D) serves to weaken most seriously the conclusion that Jencsik's budgets caused the intense growth in state spending. (E) is not the best choice; simply stating that the previous governor was said to have introduced some "budget austerity" packages does not weaken the argument that Jencsik's budgets caused intense growth in state spending.

12. **(E)** No direct claim is made in the ad for the superiority of either cotton or rayon; (A) is not the best choice. Joining the bandwagon is not the overwhelming reason that most persons would buy Swabbies after reading this advertisement. Most people are not doctors, so the advertisement does not imply that most people use Swabbies, thus (B) is a poor choice. The advertisement does not sound like one usually found in a medical journal. From the information given the reader has no idea if it is placed where those with a high degree of education and status would read it, so (C) is not the best choice. No direct statement or implication suggests that Swabbies helped the doctors attain their professional status; therefore, (D) is not the best choice. (E) is the best choice. Most readers would purchase the cotton swabs because of the transfer propaganda technique. "If a doctor recommends it, it must be right," they might conclude.

13. **(E)** Adjusting the population downward would not necessarily result in a family with an income below the median family income being able to afford the $140,000 home; (A) should not be chosen. It is very unlikely that a person with an income of only $28,000 could realistically purchase a $140,000 home. Decreasing the income, then, would not obtain the end result. So (B) is incorrect. (C) is evidently not the best choice; raising the price of the home would not help

families with an income below $56,000 to be able to purchase the home. Reducing the mortgage rate .2 of one percent would not accomplish the purpose sought — enabling families with incomes below the median family income to afford the $140,000 home; therefore, (D) is incorrect. (E) is the best choice. By pushing the amount to be spent on home payments to 32% from 25% would logically enable families with a median family income below $56,000 to purchase a $140,000 home. (Realistically, however, this may be too great of a proportion of their income for housing.)

14. **(E)**   The argument for nuclear winter rests upon an analogy: the similarity between dust storms on Mars and debris stirred up by a nuclear war on Earth. The statement that would tend most to weaken this argument is the statement that attacks this analogy. (E) is the correct choice because it attacks the analogy by denying that conditions on Mars and Earth are truly comparable. According to (E) the lack of water on Mars makes for fundamentally different atmospheric conditions. This in turn casts doubt on the validity of the comparison. If atmospheric conditions are fundamentally different, then the effects of dust on Mars might not be the same as the effects of a similar amount of debris in the Earth's atmosphere.

The other choices do not attack the argument directly. (A) and (B) concern the likelihood of a nuclear war occurring at all. This is irrelevant. The argument concerns what would happen *if* there is a nuclear war. In the argument the nuclear war is a given. Whether or not a nuclear war is likely to occur is not the question. Choice (C) concerns the likelihood of surviving a nuclear war. A nuclear winter would no doubt decrease the likelihood of survival, but whether or not survival itself is at all possible does not directly bear on the likelihood of nuclear winter. As for (D), the absence of life on Mars is not relevant. The conditions observed on Mars concern the effect of atmospheric dust on surface temperature. This effect does not depend on the existence of life on Mars. The argument is an analogy between this circumstance and a hypothetically similar circumstance on Earth.

15. **(A)**   Choice (E) is irrelevant. A mere accusation proves nothing, and in any case the mayor's political virtue has no bearing on the merits of the argument. If the accusations were proven true we might question the character of the mayor and his fitness to serve, but this is an attack on the arguer not the argument. The other statements may have some bearing on the question. (D) indicates the importance of crime as an issue. We do not know from this, however, whether raising the salaries of the police will have any effect on crime. (C) indicates that an increase is financially feasible, but not that it is necessarily appropriate. The

surplus might just as well be spent on something else or returned to the taxpayers. The significance of (B) depends on the relative value to be placed on the different jobs of police officers and fire fighters. This is certainly a matter of potential debate, but not one that could be resolved without further information. With nothing more to go on, we have no reason to assume that the salaries should be different.

When we turn, however, to choice (A), we see that it has a direct bearing on the mayor's argument. The mayor refers to a 10% increase over the last five years. What this means is directly affected by the information in statement (A). A 3% annual rate of inflation adds up to a 15% rate of inflation over the five-year period. Thus the real income of the police officers, the buying power of their salaries, has actually been decreasing. In the light of this information, the mayor's argument is not very persuasive, and an increase in salaries would seem to be appropriate.

16. **(D)** One cannot tell from the information given if Lorenzo is older than Nedino. One knows that Lorenzo is older than Martin, but he could still be younger than Nedino. On the other hand, he could be older than Nedino, so (A) is not the best choice. One knows that Lorenzo is older than Martin, but one does not know how Lorenzo ranks in relation to Juarez. (C) also cannot be stated as truth. One knows that Korrie and Nedino are twins. One also knows that Martin is younger than Nedino and that Lorenzo is older than Martin. The reader, however, is not told for sure how Lorenzo ranks in relation to the others. (D) is the right choice. Juarez is older than Korrie; Korrie and Nedino are twins. Since Martin is younger than Nedino, he is also younger than Korrie. Since the reader is told that Martin is younger than Nedino and since Korrie and Nedino are twins, Martin is younger than Korrie. (E), however, states that Korrie is younger than Martin and is incorrect.

17. **(C)** The problem here is to grasp the basic idea expressed in the opening statement and then determine how this general notion applies to the specific examples in the three statements: I, II, and III. The basic idea is that a particular institutional policy may help one group associated with the institution while hurting another group associated with the institution. The first statement (I) illustrates the idea in that the increase in faculty salaries helps one group, the faculty, but hurts another group, the students, because it results in lan increase in tutoring. The second statement (II) illustrates the idea in that the policy, a decrease in fees, helps one group, the patients, but hurts another group, the nurses, because it results in lower wages for the nursing staff. The third statement (III) does *not* illustrate the idea. Adding to the fund-raising staff results, according to the statement, in an increase in money available for scholarships.

Since the added fund-raising effort increases the total amount of money available to the institution, it does not take from one group in order to give to another group. Thus, in terms of the institution, no one is hurt by the policy. The correct choice is thus (C). Statement I and II support the claim, while statement III does not.

18. **(A)** In the opening statement we are told that the number of elderly is increasing more rapidly than the number of wage earners, and the cost of caring for the elderly will have to come from the incomes of the wage earners. Since the ratio of elderly to wage earners is increasing, it follows that, other things being equal, each wage earner will have to pay a higher percentage of his or her income for care of the elderly. This assumes that average income does not increase enough to make up the difference.

The other choices are all possibilities, but they do not follow directly from the information given. Thus (B), (C), and (E) are contingent upon (D). Whether the elderly receive adequate care, whether only the rich receive adequate care, and whether citizens would be advised to start saving their own funds to provide for their own needs all depend at least in part on the willingness of future wage earners to pay the taxes needed to care for the elderly. There is nothing in the statement that implies that voters in the future will or will not vote for such taxes.

19. **(D)** If for the poor person the 5% sales tax is equivalent to an income tax "close to or at 5%," then it follows that the poor person spends all or almost all of his or her income. If, on the other hand, for the rich person the same sales tax is equivalent to a much lower percentage of his or her income, then it follows that the rich person spends a much lower percentage of his or her income. Presumably the rich person saves more than the poor person, both absolutely and as a percentage of their income. Thus we can infer (D) "Poor people spend a larger percentage of their income than rich people" from the passage.

As for the other statements, they cannot be inferred directly from the passage. One might assume (A), but it is not necessarily implied. One must first assume that the rich person is spending at least as much as the poor person. This seems like a reasonable assumption, but it is not stated or implied in the passage. (B) also depends on additional information. The truth of (B) would depend on the definitions of "rich" and "poor" and the total numbers falling into each category. None of this information is given in the passage. (C) is a notion extraneous to the passage. Nothing is said or implied about finding ways to avoid paying taxes. (E) is a quasi-moral judgment about who should pay what. The assumption that calling a sales tax "regressive" is a criticism implies that the tax should be at least flat: an equal percentage of income. Thus, (E) is compatible with the argument as a whole but it is not implied by the specific example. The question asks for a statement implied by the passage. Furthermore, the passage assumes that a regressive tax is undesirable, but does not state or imply *why* it is undesirable. Thus (E) is consistent with, but not implied by, the passage.

20. **(B)** During the previous governor's administration the budget increased 12%; the rate of inflation was 10%. This meant the cost was actually 2%. Taylor's budget increase was 6%; the rate of inflation was 4%. This cost was actually 2%, the same as the previous governor's. Statement (A) with 2% for the previous governor and 2% for Taylor does not support the conclusion. The previous governor's budget was 12% with an inflation rate of 9%; the cost was 3%. Taylor's increase was 6% with an inflation rate of 1%; the cost was 5%. This cost rate seems to support the conclusion that Taylor did not control state spending; therefore, (B) is the correct choice. "Some increase in spending" does not seriously support the conclusion that Taylor did not control state spending; (C) is not the best choice. Having individuals take over the payment for numerous services seems an indication that Taylor was trying to control state spending. (D) does not support the conclusion that Taylor's actions did not fit his promises. The fact that the previous governor introduced some "austerity" measures does not support the conclusion that Taylor did not control state spending, so (E) is certainly not the best choice.

21. **(A)** Since the opponents of prison reform did, in fact, attack the character of the inmates rather than their claims, (A) is the best choice. The opponents of prison reform were not reported to have referred to the analogy; (B) is not the best choice. No dilemma was implied by opponents of the prison reform; (C) is not the best choice. No absurd conclusion was brought out by the opponents, therefore, (D) should not be selected. The opponents to prison reform skirted the issue of prison riots in a neighboring county, (E) is not the best choice.

22. **(A)** Of the choices given, the best defense of the former prison inmates would be to emphasize their expertise and the expertise of those who invited them to the meeting; thus, (A) is the best choice. Getting into a discussion of their character would not help the situation; (B) is not the best choice. Denying that changes would cost money which would necessitate a tax increase would be a false argument, so (C) should not be selected. Again, bringing up the riots might sound like a threat; (D) would not defend the inmate's position. There is no point in the former inmates' refuting their own analogy; (E) is not the best choice.

23. **(D)** No claim is made in the advertisement that Good Health is the most nutritionally complete: (A) is incorrect. Although reference is made to the fact that accomplished or professional athletes reading the *Bulletin* prefer Good Health,

(B) is not the most obvious claim. Since health is a concern of all people, there is nothing in the ad to suggest that only accomplished or professional athletes would read the *Bulletin*,;therefore, (C) is incorrect. (D) is probably the reason that most persons who are not accomplished or professional would choose the product — to receive the help (implied in the ad) which helped the athletes to become accomplished or professional. (E) is not the best choice. No suggestion is made that only those who will become accomplished or professional subscribe to the *Bulletin* or will read the ad.

24. **(E)**   Finding a skeleton 1.6 million years old which so closely resembles the human form confirmsd that the human form is *quite* old. Hence, (A) is incorrect. There is no evidence that the remains may have confused two different time periods; (B) is incorrrect. No evidence suggests that the body fell down a gerbil hole, so (C) is incorrect. The passage makes no mention of religious groups using human sacrifices; (D) is incorrect. (E) is the correct choice. This body confirms the antiquity of the human form.

25. **(C)**   (A) is not the best choice. Most scientists believed that humans existed 1.6 million years ago; they were not sure that these humans looked as much like humans today as the skeletal remains indicated. (B) should not be selected; there was no magic date like 100 B.C., according to the passage, when humans looked like humans. (C) is the best choice. It was a surprise to most scientists that the skeletal remains for a child were the size and proportion that they were. The discovery seems to indicated that humans reached their present size more than a million and a half years ago; the smaller size was a result of populations in poor areas. (D) is not the best choice; the discovery *abolished* the belief that humans have grown larger through time. (E) should not be chosen since the passage does not support the belief that human life began on the continent of Europe.

26. **(E)**   If surgery to disconnect the two sides of the brain results in both sides of the brain working well, the theory that the two sides work together would not necessarily be substantiated. Hence, (A) would not strengthen their argument and should not be selected. Since the right hemisphere is not believed to control logic, damage to it would not result in logical disorders being manifested, (B) would not strengthen the position of opponents to the split-brain theory. Opponents of the split-brain theory contend that both hemispheres of the brain work together; hence, an activity would generally engage both hemispheres of the brain — not just one as (C) implies. The hemispheres, opponents of the split-brain theory argue, work together — not independently as (D) implies. Opponents of the split-brain theory *would* argue that it is impossible to educate one side of the brain without educating the other, making (E) the best choice.

27. **(E)** If the people had drowned and the bodies washed into the crevices, dirt, sand, and sediment would have been embedded in their clothes; (A) is not the best choice. If the people had died of starvation, there would have been evidence of gnawing on the animal skins in which they were dressed. (B) is not the correct choice. Since the skins of the people were not disfigured, smallpox would not have been the cause of death; (C) is not the correct choice. Since the bodies had been placed there at different times, the people could not have frozen to death; (D) is not the best choice. The scientists decided that the dead had to have been placed there by family members. (E) is the correct answer.

28. **(B)** Since Greenland is primarily a cold area, the hot dry air would not apply; (A) is not correct. (B) is the correct answer. The cold climate and the winds preserved the bodies. (C) is inappropriate. The bodies had not recently been placed there. The passage tells the reader the date of death was around 1475. Moisture from water would not postpone deterioration but would hasten it; therefore, (D) is inappropriate. The bodies were so perfectly preserved it is unlikely that lightning would have struck the bodies. If lightning had struck the bodies, they would have been damaged. Evidence also indicated death had come at different times. (E) is incorrect.

29. **(D)** The problem here is to sort out the various factors affecting Alvin's decision. Choices (A) and (B) relate to the cost of insurance. Choice(A), an increase in the liability requirement, would increase the cost of insuring the car and thus make it more difficult for Alvin to afford the more expensive car. Choice (B), choosing the policy with the lowest deductibles, would also make it more expensive to insure the car and therefore would also make it more difficult for Alvin to buy the more expensive car. Choices (C) and (D) relate to the car loan. Choice (C), paying the lowest possible downpayment, would increase the amount of money to be borrowed and thus would increase the monthly payments. This would make it more difficult for Alvin to buy the more expensive car. Choice(D), decreasing the interest rate, would decrease the monthly payments. this would make it easier for Alvin to afford the more expensive car. As for choice (E), this would make both cars more expensive to operate. Since the subcompact gets better mileage, higher operation costs would make it more difficult for Alvin to afford the more expensive car. Thus only choice (D), lowering "the interest rate on Alvin's car loan," would make it easier for Alvin to afford the more expensive car.

30. **(D)**   A reference to a parallel three years ago between a decline in food stamps and a robust economy does not refute the author's claim; (A) is not the correct choice. The source of the funding for the food stamps is not the issue; (B) does not refute the author's claim. The relationship between population growth and a decline in food stamps issued does not refute the author's claim; (C) should not be selected. The reference to the stricter application process and the increased help needed from food kitchens is the closest reference made to refuting the author's claim. Therefore, (D) is the correct answer. The fact that all deserving people currently receive food stamps does not refute the author's claim; (E) is not the best selection.

CHAPTER 3

Logical and Critical Reasoning Review

LOGICAL AND CRITICAL REASONING REVIEW

> **Study this section for tests:**
> **GMAT, GRE, and LSAT**

Logical and Critical Reasoning Questions

The logical or critical reasoning questions on standardized tests are perhaps one of the most difficult of all the sections. (Note that the logical reasoning section is synonymous with the critical reasoning section.) These questions test thinking and logical skills rather than basic knowledge of skills such as vocabulary or grammar. Reasoning questions are difficult since we cannot practice by memorizing specific items such as a word or a phrase. Instead, we need to rely on our thinking processes.

The following review will help make the logical and critical reasoning questions less overwhelming. You will learn how to choose the correct answer by first evaluating and identifying the type of argument used in a problem. You will then learn how to approach each problem. You will not need any knowledge of formal logic or its terminology to solve the questions. Taking all the drills and the practice test will greatly increase your understanding of this section so you will be able to take the logical or critical reasoning tests with confidence and proficiency.

Basically, the reasoning questions are based on an argument or set of statements. The questions will ask you to evaluate the argument and then draw conclusions and, sometimes, identify underlying assumptions based on the argument.

ARGUMENTS

Let's take a look at the parts of an argument. The three basic parts are a premise, the reasoning, and a conclusion. A **premise** is the reason or evidence which an author gives to support his or her position. Unstated premises are **assumptions**. **Reasoning** is the way in which the author uses his or her premises to support the conclusion he or she is trying to prove. The conclusion is the point of the argument and is sometimes left unstated.

The arguments generally follow two basic patterns:

1. premise, premise, premise, conclusion

2. conclusion, premise, premise, premise

The critical or logical reasoning section incorporates examples of different types of reasoning with which you should be familiar.

Deductive reasoning and inductive reasoning are the most common types of arguments. **Deductive reasoning** basically requires you to ask yourself, "If premises X, Y, and Z are true, which conclusions MUST therefore be true?" When you reason deductively, you move from a **generalization to something specific**.

Inductive reasoning requires you to ask yourself, "If premises X, Y, and Z are true, which conclusions are therefore PROBABLE?" Inductive reasoning is more vague than deductive reasoning because it calls for a generalization based on a limited specific experience. In inductive reasoning, you move from **specific items to a generalization**. This will be discussed in detail later in the review.

There are nine basic types of logical and critical reasoning questions. Each of the questions requires you to perform one of the following logical operations.

1. Questions that ask you to determine the main point or conclusion of an argument

2. Questions that ask you to detect the underlying assumption of an argument

3. Questions that ask you to form a conclusion based on the premises or evidence provided

4. Questions that ask you to identify the principles being applied in the passage and apply those principles to a different case

5. Questions that ask you to determine the method of argument or persuasion being used

6. Questions that ask you to find errors and misinterpretations in the argument

7. Questions that ask you to evaluate the strength of the argument

8. Questions that ask you to determine how additional information would affect the argument given

9. Questions that ask you to assess whether the conclusion is consistent with the argument which is made to support it

Locating Premises and Conclusions

To do well on logical reasoning tests, you must be able to locate the premises and conclusions in the arguments. In some arguments, this is easy because the premises are given first and are followed by the conclusion. This is not always true. Sometimes the conclusion comes first, followed by the premises.

EXAMPLE

Bill will not be able to change the oil in his car. To change the oil, he needs a wrench for removing the drain plug, and he does not have one.

In this example the conclusion comes first, followed by the premises. We could make this argument conform to the standard pattern:

Major premise: To change the oil in a car, one must have a wrench to remove the drain plug.

Minor premise: Bill does not have a wrench.

Conclusion: Bill will not be able to change the oil in his car.

The premises appear first and the conclusion appears last. The logic of the argument remains the same.

What is the Author Trying to Prove?

One way to determine which statements are premises and which is the conclusion is to ask yourself what the author is trying to prove. Remember, the conclusion is what the author wants to prove, and the premises are the assumptions which support the conclusion.

EXAMPLE

Ann got bonus points on her assignment because she turned it in early, and all assignments turned in early received bonus points.

What is the author trying to prove? That Ann turned her assignment in early? No. If that was the author's purpose, we would expect something like this: "The assignments were due on Thursday, but Ann turned hers in on Wednesday. Therefore, she turned it in early." If the author wanted to show that early assignments got bonus points, we would expect something like: "Mr. Simms said that all early assignments would receive bonus points." However, we do not see either of these statements supported by argument or evidence. They are the assumptions or premises of the argument. What we do see are statements that support the idea that Ann got bonus points. We know, then, that Ann got bonus points is the conclusion. The author is trying to prove that assignments turned in early get bonus points.

Linguistic Indicators

Many times the premises and conclusion may be determined by what may be termed linguistic indicators, words which indicate the function of a phrase or sentence within an argument. Premise indicators include:

…proves	…implies
…shows	…means
…establishes	

The three dots before each word represent the premise. With the words above, the premise will precede the linguistic indicator. Sometimes, however, the premise will follow an indicator:

since…	inasmuch as…
because…	seeing that…
for…	insofar as

Conclusion indicators include:

accordingly…	which means that…
as a result…	which proves that…
so…	it can be inferred that…

it follows that…   therefore…

consequently…   hence…

which shows that…   thus.…

Uncovering Hidden (Unstated) Premises

Some logical reasoning questions will ask you to find the underlying assumption of an argument. The underlying assumption is a hidden or unstated premise of an argument. An unstated premise, in turn, is one that must be true for the argument to be valid.

EXAMPLE

This is purple passion perfume, so it must be expensive.

The explicit premise is that this is purple passion perfume. The explicit conclusion is that this perfume must be expensive. The conclusion does not follow logically from the given premise. What is left out, then, is the premise that purple passion perfume is expensive. The complete argument is:

Major premise (unstated): Purple passion perfume is expensive.

Minor premise (stated):   This is purple passion perfume.

Conclusion: This perfume is expensive.

Whenever a logical reasoning question asks you to identify an unstated premise, you should read the passage carefully, asking yourself "What is necessary for the argument to be valid?"

Strengthening or Weakening Arguments

There is another type of question which appears often on logical reasoning tests and is closely related to finding hidden premises. This type of question asks you to identify the statement which either strengthens or weakens the conclusion drawn in the passage. When the question calls for the answer choice that weakens the argument, the answer will be one which undermines a hidden premise. When the question calls for the answer choice that strengthens the conclusion, the answer will be one which supports a hidden premise.

Suggested Strategies

➤ Determine first exactly what the question is asking. It may be helpful to read the question first before reading the given statements or passage.

➤ When reading the set of given statements or passage, focus on the factual information, what is implied from the statements, and how well the conclusion from the statements is substantiated.

➤ Look for themes in the first and last sentences of passages. That's where they usually are.

➤ Use the process of elimination to weed out choices.

➤ Read the passages carefully for ideas.

➤ Ask yourself what the author is trying to convince you of.

Drill: Arguments

DIRECTIONS: The questions in this section are based on the reasoning contained in brief statements or passages. For some questions, more than one of the choices could conceivably answer the question. However, you are to choose the **best** answer; that is, the response that most accurately and completely answers the question. You should not make assumptions that are by common-sense standards implausible, superfluous, or incompatible with the passage.

1. Karen checked the costume and found no sewing mistakes. Therefore, the costume had no sewing mistakes.

    Which of the following is an unspoken assumption of the argument?

    (A)   The costume is a good replica of the clothes of the time period covered in the play.

    (B)   The seamstress who sewed the costume has sewed many such costumes without making any sewing mistakes.

    (C)   Karen sewed the costume herself.

    (D)   Karen is a professional seamstress.

    (E)   Karen never fails to find sewing mistakes in costumes.

2. Contrary to popular perceptions, rock climbing is a very safe sport. The number of people who die each year rock climbing is about the same as the number of people who die each year bicycling. And the number of people who die each year bicycling is nearly the same as the number of people who die each year jogging. So the fact is, rock climbing is no more dangerous than bicycling or jogging.

    Which of the following, if true, would most seriously weaken the author's conclusion?

    (A)   Statistics show that many more people jog and bicycle than rock climb.

(B) The number of bicyclists killed each year is very small only because there are laws governing the use of the roads.

(C) Jogging is among the safest forms of physical exercise. Were the author to compare fatalities from skydiving, the number would be much higher.

(D) Most people would much rather take their chances jogging and bicycling than they would rock climbing.

(E) All forms of mountaineering, taken together, kill many more people than are killed by cars while bicycling or jogging.

Questions 3 and 4 are based on the following.

Since the planets revolve around the sun in orbits like the paths of electrons revolving around the nucleus of an atom, why couldn't our whole solar system just be an atom in the tail of a dog wagging in some much larger universe?

3. The author bases his argument for a "larger universe" on

(A) an implied analogy between the universe and an atom.

(B) evidence of life on other planets.

(C) the theory of the expanding universe.

(D) an implied analogy between the solar system and an atom.

(E) the fact that the sun is the ultimate source of all energy on the Earth.

4. A major weakness in the author's argument for a "larger universe" would be that

(A) there is no real evidence of life on other planets.

(B) the only similarity between the solar system and an atom is one of superficial form.

(C) no one can actually see an atom, so no one really knows what atoms look like.

(D)   no one has yet travelled further away than the moon, so we do not know much about the solar system.

(E)   there is no reason to believe that a "larger universe" would be inhabited by a dog.

5.   Research indicates that individuals who have served in the Peace Corps tend to be more radical politically than other citizens of the same age. Obviously, the experience of serving in the Peace Corps had a radicalizing influence on these individuals.

Which of the following, if true, would most strengthen the conclusion?

(A)   Individuals who volunteer for the Peace Corps are more knowledgeable than other citizens on questions of geography.

(B)   Individuals who have served in the Peace Corps are more tolerant of ethnic and cultural differences than are other citizens.

(C)   The research also indicated that those who did not serve in the Peace Corps were more interested in making money.

(D)   Peace Corps volunteers, but not the other individuals, probably realized that the questions they were asked related to the political influence of the Peace Corps experience.

(E)   Individuals who volunteer for the Peace Corps are not more radical than other citizens prior to serving in the Peace Corps.

Arguments
Detailed Explanations
of Answers

1.   **(E)**   Hidden Assumption. The answer to the question is (E). If we are to conclude that the costume has no sewing mistakes because Karen failed to find any, then we must assume that Karen never misses any mistakes that might exist. Choice (A) is beside the point, since the passage says nothing about the costume being a replica of the clothes of any time period. Choice (B) might support the conclusion that the costume has no sewing mistakes, but it doesn't help us to understand how the author of the passage concludes there are no mistakes based on Karen's examination of the costume. Choice (C) fails to explain how Karen's examination of the costume is authoritative with regard to there being no mistakes. Choice (D) is the strongest alternative to (E). It fails, however, because it is not necessary to assume that Karen is a professional seamstress in order to reach the conclusion. What is necessary is the simple assumption that had there been a mistake, she would have found it.

2.   **(A)**   Weakening Argument. The author argues that rock climbing is no more dangerous than bicycling or jogging. His proof is that no more people are killed rock climbing than doing either of the other two. (For his argument to be strong, it must be true that just as many people rock climb as jog or bicycle.) If a thousand times as many people jog and bicycle as rock climb, but the same number are killed in each of the three activities, it would follow that rock climbing is a thousand times more dangerous. Therefore, the correct answer is (A). Choice (B), even if true, would have no effect on the argument. It makes no difference WHY the number of bicyclists killed each year is small, so long as the numbers killed in each activity are about the same. Choice (C) might actually strengthen the author's argument. If jogging is a safe sport, and the same number are killed jogging and rock climbing, then rock climbing may also be relatively safe. The author is not dealing with people's preferences, but rather is trying to establish that rock climbing is as safe as jogging or bicycling. Therefore, what people prefer to do, (D), is beside the point.

3.   **(D)**   Analogy. The comparison between the atom and the solar system is correctly identified as an analogy. Whether or not there is life on other planets, whether or not the sun is the source of all energy, and whether or not the universe is expanding are all extraneous to this argument. Choice (A) correctly identifies the argument as an analogy, but incorrectly identifies the terms of the comparison.

The argument compares the atom, not with the universe as a whole, but only with the solar system. Thus, (D) is the correct answer, identifying the argument as an analogy and identifying the terms of the analogy as an atom and the solar system.

4. **(B)**   Analogy. Arguments by analogy stress the similarity of two things that may otherwise be quite unalike. Such is the case in this particular argument. Although the form of the atom and the form of the solar system are similar, there seems to be no other basis for the comparison and therefore no reason to assume any further similarities. Whether or not there is life on other planets (A) is irrelevant to the argument. What we know about the world is not limited to our immediate visual field so (C) would not weaken the argument. Similarly, what we know about the solar system is not limited simply by human space travel so (D) is not an issue. The example of the dog's tail is just an entertaining image not necessary to the argument itself (E). Thus, the problem is to identify the essential weakness of the argument. This essential weakness is expressed in (B): the comparison focuses entirely on one superficial similarity while ignoring many basic differences.

5. **(E)**   Strengthening Argument. The problem with the argument is that the conclusion may follow, but does not necessarily follow, from the evidence. The evidence shows a difference between two groups of people: Peace Corps and non-Peace Corps. The former are more radical than the latter. The conclusion *assumes* that this difference is a result of serving in the Peace Corps. It might not be. Perhaps the Peace Corps volunteers were more radical to start with and that is why they volunteered. This possibility would be ruled out by (E), and therefore (E) would strengthen the conclusion. The other arguments are irrelevant. Knowledge of geography (A), tolerance of ethnic and cultural differences (B), a desire or lack of desire to make money (C) might be acquired through Peace Corps service or might be present already in the volunteers before their service. In any case, it is not clear just how these factors would relate to a radical political point of view. As for (D), this would certainly weaken the argument rather than strengthen it, since it would suggest a contamination of the evidence. If one group realized that they were being tested and the other group did not, then this awareness might affect the answers given.

DEDUCTIVE ARGUMENTS

Deductive arguments are those whose premises are intended to provide absolute proof of the conclusion. Deductive arguments move from general premises to specific conclusions.

EXAMPLE

Major premise: All whales are mammals.

Minor premise: Orca is a whale.

Conclusion: Orca is a mammal.

In this example, the conclusion follows of necessity from the premises. If all whales are mammals, then any given whale will be a mammal. The example above is also called a SYLLOGISM. A syllogism is a deductive argument with a major premise, a minor premise, and a conclusion.

A deductive argument is considered VALID when the inference from the premises is a necessary one. If whales are mammals and Orca is a whale, then Orca must be a mammal.

A deductive argument may be valid, but not true. Such a deductive argument is referred to as an "unsound" argument. An unsound argument occurs when one of the premises is false, but the conclusion follows necessarily from the argument.

EXAMPLE

Major premise: All whales are cold-blooded.

Minor premise: Orca is a whale.

Conclusion: Orca is cold-blooded.

This is a valid argument. If all whales are cold-blooded, and Orca is a whale, then of necessity Orca must be cold-blooded. However, the conclusion cannot be true, since the major premise is false.

When taking logical reasoning tests it will be important for you to remember the difference between valid and invalid deductive arguments, and sound and unsound deductive arguments. Sometimes you will be given a passage which contains a valid but unsound deductive argument. You will then be asked to choose the answer which contains the same type of argument. Don't waste time forming objections to the arguments. Simply identify the mistake and look for the answer which makes the same type of mistake.

INDUCTIVE ARGUMENTS

Inductive arguments differ from deductive arguments in that the inference involved in getting from the premises to the conclusion is a probable, not a necessary, one. Inductive arguments involve an interpretation of some experience or experiences.

Inductive arguments move from specific premises to general observations.

EXAMPLE

Premise: The sun came up today, yesterday, and every previous day of my life.

Conclusion: The sun will come up every succeeding day of my life.

As you can see, the argument is based on experience. The conclusion does not follow with absolute certainty. There may be a time in which the sun will not come up anymore. It may be tomorrow. However, it is very probable that the sun will come up tomorrow and every other day of our lives.

Inductive arguments deal with probabilities. Their conclusions are more or less probable based on the supporting evidence. Inductive arguments are termed stronger or weaker depending on the probability of the conclusion.

EXAMPLE

Premise: Jill Black has used her electric can opener thousands of times, and it has never malfunctioned.

Conclusion: Therefore, it won't give her any problem with the can she's now opening.

This argument is invalid, since the conclusion does not follow, even if we assume the premise to be true. But notice that, even though the conclusion may be false, it is UNLIKELY that it is false. This is a strong argument because, given that the premise is true, it is unlikely that the conclusion is false.

We could rewrite the passage about Jill Black to produce a weak argument.

EXAMPLE

Jill Black's new can opener didn't give her any problem on the first can, so it will open thousands of cans without malfunctioning.

This argument is weak, because it is dangerous to make such a generalization on the basis of such scant experience.

Drill: Deductive and Inductive Arguments

> **DIRECTIONS**: The questions in this section are based on the reasoning contained in brief statements or passages. For some questions, more than one of the choices could conceivably answer the question. However, you are to choose the **best** answer; that is, the response that most accurately and completely answers the question. You should not make assumptions that are by common-sense standards implausible, superfluous, or incompatible with the passage.

1. All bird dogs instinctively hunt pheasants. English setters are bird dogs. Therefore, Rover, an English setter, will hunt pheasants.

   Which of the following has a logical structure most like the logical structure of the argument above?

   (A) I have had three pairs of Wilcot shoes, all of which have been comfortable. Therefore, all Wilcot shoes are comfortable.

   (B) The tree you just transplanted will not live, because I have transplanted many trees this time of year, and they all died.

   (C) Studies show that great athletes generally do cross-training. If you want to be a good basketball player, you should play baseball this spring.

   (D) All Tiaras have air-cooled engines. Your new car is a Tiara, therefore, it has an air-cooled engine.

   (E) A majority of people surveyed preferred brand Y over brand X. Therefore, brand Y is a better buy.

2. Which of the following draws a conclusion about a group that is based upon a fact about its individual members?

   (A) The office staff all go to Al's Grill for lunch. Therefore, we can find Lynn, the secretary, there at 12:00.

   (B) I didn't like the looks of the red Camaro. When I buy one it will be blue.

   (C) That chili tastes good. Therefore, the beans, peppers, and tomato sauce from which it is made also taste good.

   (D) Each of the threads in the blouse is monochrome. Therefore, the blouse is monochrome.

   (E) You can't trust Ed's advice on the stock market. He is a broker, and all they want to do is make a sale to get their commission.

3. Israel's present system of high taxes, low wages, and a tortuous bureaucracy stifles initiative, but it also makes us better fathers. Israel's inefficient economy and relative lack of economic opportunity prevent most Israelis from sacrificing family values for the material rewards of financial success. True success to an Israeli father is getting the kids out the door each morning feeling good about themselves.

   What is the main reason offered in this passage for the claim that Israelis are better fathers?

   (A) Lack of economic opportunity allows Israelis to focus on family values rather than on material gain.

   (B) Israeli children feel good about themselves.

   (C) Israelis have economic opportunities that allow them material rewards of financial success.

   (D) Israelis have no initiative to reduce high taxes.

   (E) Israelis have a tortuous democracy.

4. As Lockard points out, frustration is a function of two related factors. The first is the perception that secured rights may be lost in the future. The second is the perception that future advancement (be it economic, social, or political) is artificially limited by factors other than a man's ability or skill. This condition is the crux of the Kern Commission's

indictment of white America and forms the basis for the continuing frustration and alienation of the black man in America today.

Which of the following is not one of the assumptions of this argument?

(A) Lockard is correct.

(B) Future advancement is limited by man's ability or skill.

(C) The Kern Commission found fault with white America.

(D) Rights considered secured are not guaranteed.

(E) The black man in America is alienated.

5.   There is no need to spend much time demonstrating that Molière had contact with, and was affected by, Italian forms of comic theatre. That such influences were constantly available to him is a commonplace rather than a point of contention. Let just two facts stand for a host of others, so that we may dispose of the point. From 1658 to 1660 Molière's company shared their acting space with a resident Italian troupe. Secondly, his personal acting style was seen by contemporaries to have been modelled to some extent on that of Tiberio Fiorilli.

Which statement, if true, would weaken the writer's argument?

(A) Molière's company shared acting space with a resident Italian troupe until 1665, not 1660.

(B) There were several forms of comic theatre in Italy.

(C) Molière's acting troupe was very small.

(D) There are other facts which the writer could note to help demonstrate his point.

(E) Tiberio Fiorilli was born and raised in Argentina.

Deductive and
Inductive Arguments
Detailed Explanations
of Answers

1.   **(D)**   Deductive Argument. The passage uses a deductive argument to reach its conclusion. It reasons from the general premise that all bird dogs hunt pheasants, to the specific conclusion that a particular bird dog will hunt pheasants. You must look for the answer choice which also uses a deductive approach. (A) is an inductive argument. It reaches the general conclusion that all Wilcot shoes share a characteristic (comfort) from the particular experience of three pairs of those shoes. Choice (B) uses the same type of argument, that since something has happened several times it will happen again. Choice (C) is the same type of argument in a slightly different form. Any time a study is cited, an inductive argument is being used. Studies examine individual members of a group and try to generalize from the findings about those individuals. All of the great athletes studied do cross-training, so the generalization is that cross-training is a key to being a great athlete. Choice (D) is a deductive argument. It starts from the major premise that all members of a class have characteristic A, so any member of the class must have that characteristic. This is the form of argument used in the main passage, so (D) is the answer. Choice (E) is very similar to choice (C). Since a majority of people surveyed prefer brand Y, we generalize that it must be the better buy.

2.   **(D)**   Inductive Argument. This question asks you to look for the answer which: (1) states a fact about the members of some group; (2) concludes that, because the fact is true of the individual members, it is true of the group which the members comprise. Choice (A) uses the opposite approach to what the question asks for. It concludes that a member of a group, Lynn, will be somewhere at a certain time, because the group as a whole is there at that time. Instead of extrapolating from a fact known about the members to a conclusion about the group, it extrapolates from the group to a particular member. Choice (B) draws no conclusions about Camaros as a whole, based on particular Camaros. It speaks only of a red Camaro and a blue one. Choice (C) states a fact about the group, chili, and draws a conclusion about the members based on that fact. This is just the opposite of what you are to look for. Choice (D) states a fact

about the members of a group, and draws a conclusion about the group based on that fact. Of course, the argument is flawed. But you were not asked to identify a flaw in the argument, but to identify a certain type of argument. Choice (E) draws a conclusion about Ed, a member of a group, based on a statement about the group as a whole.

3. **(A)** Identifying Premises. The conclusion of the passage is that Israeli fathers are exceptionally good fathers. The main reason, or premise, is that Israel's economy is so poor, that Israelis have no incentive to pursue economic gains. This lack of interest permits Israeli fathers to focus on family values (A). Choice (B) illustrates the goodness of the Israeli father, but is not the main reason why these fathers are good. By claiming that Israelis have good economic opportunities, choice (C) contradicts the main premise of the passage. The passage does not claim that Israelis have no initiative to reduce high taxes (D) or that Israelis have a tortuous democracy (E).

4. **(B)** Inductive Argument. The writer agrees with Lockard (A) that black men are frustrated and alienated (E), because, in part, they feel insecure about their rights (D) and they feel their further advance is limited by factors having nothing to do with their abilities or skills. The writer also cites the Kern Commission's indictment of white America (C) as support for his argument. The writer neither suggests nor assumes that further advancement is limited by man's ability or skill (B).

5. **(E)** Deductive Argument. The argument that Molière was influenced by Italian forms of comic opera is based on the premises that Molière's company shared space with an Italian troupe and that Molière allegedly modelled his acting style on Tiberio Fiorilli. The assumption in the second premise is that Fiorilli was Italian, so if he was Argentinian (E), this would weaken the argument. If Molière's troupe shared acting space with Italians for seven years instead of two (A), this would strengthen the argument, not weaken it. Whether or not there were several forms of comic theatre in Italy (B) is irrelevant to the premises that an Italian troupe and an Italian actor influenced Molière. Choice (C) is also irrelevant, since the argument is about Molière, not about his troupe or the size of his troupe. That other facts might strengthen the argument (D), does not necessarily make the argument weaker as it stands—the current premises might make the argument sufficiently probable to make further help unnecessary.

FORMS OF LOGICAL OR CRITICAL REASONING ARGUMENTS

The following are some common types of logical/critical reasoning questions found on standardized tests.

Type	Description	Example
I. Deductive	Argues from general to specific, to PROVE the argument which may be VALID though not true.	Adult humans have 32 teeth. Joe is an adult human. Therefore, Joe has 32 teeth.
A. Categorical	Describes relationships of classes or categories.	No redheads are on the team. Some brunettes are on the team. Some brunettes are tall. Therefore, no redheads are tall.
B. Categorical Using Venn Diagrams	Venn diagrams are visual representations of categorical arguments and may help solve the problem.	

1. All members are men.

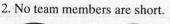

M = men
T = team

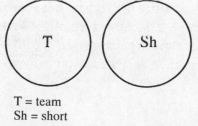

2. No team members are short.

T = team
Sh = short

Type	Description	Example
		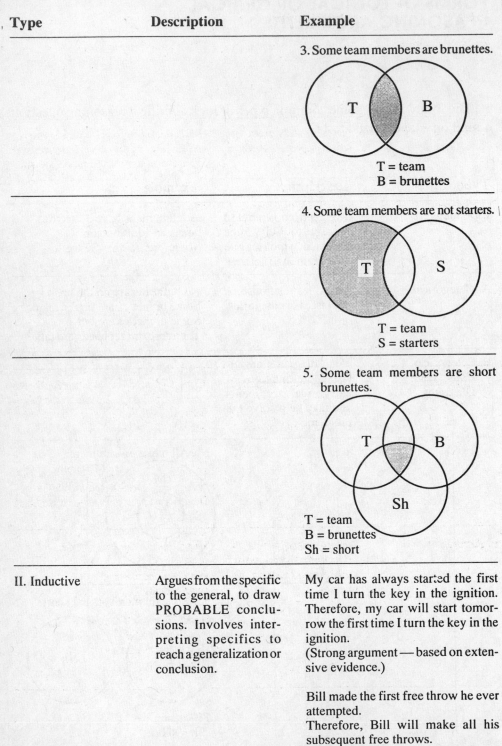 3. Some team members are brunettes. T = team B = brunettes
		4. Some team members are not starters. T = team S = starters
		5. Some team members are short brunettes. T = team B = brunettes Sh = short
II. Inductive	Argues from the specific to the general, to draw PROBABLE conclusions. Involves interpreting specifics to reach a generalization or conclusion.	My car has always started the first time I turn the key in the ignition. Therefore, my car will start tomorrow the first time I turn the key in the ignition. (Strong argument — based on extensive evidence.) Bill made the first free throw he ever attempted. Therefore, Bill will make all his subsequent free throws. (Weak argument — based on little evidence.)

Type	Description	Example
A. Generalization	A characteristic of one member of a class is said to apply to, or characterize, all members of the class.	This lemon pie is too sour. So I'll never eat lemon pie again.
B. Causal Argument	A cause-and-effect relationship is set forth: x causes y.	I felt happy before I saw the movie. After the show I felt depressed. Therefore, the movie made me sad.
C. Circular Reasoning	An argument in which what the author is trying to prove is used as a premise in the proof.	Larry is insane. He just did something crazy. Therefore, he's insane. Mugs is a criminal. The guys he hangs out with are criminals. They're criminals because anyone who'd hang out with Mugs must be a criminal.
D. Ad Hominen Argument	An argument attacked on the basis of the character of its author, not on its own merits.	Copernicus' idea that the earth revolves around the sun cannot be taken seriously because, as everyone knows, Copernicus cheats on his taxes. Candidate Smith's economic policy will never work because he is believed to have had an extramarital affair.
E. Ambiguity	An argument which is undermined by vague or ambiguous words or phrases.	Happiness is the end of life. (end = goal?) (end = termination?) (end = death?) X: Joe is a big TV fan. Y: Oh no, Joe isn't at all fat. (big = enthusiastic?) (big = fat?)

COMMON FORMS OF DEDUCTIVE ARGUMENTS

As mentioned in the chart, there are two types of Deductive Arguments: Categorical and Categorical using Venn Diagrams.

Categorical Arguments

There is one type of deductive reasoning which deserves special treatment. It is called categorical reasoning. Passages which use categorical arguments will require you to reach conclusions based on descriptions of classes or categories. There are four standard forms of categorical statements:

A. All x are y;

B. No x are y;

C. Some x are y;

D. Some x are not y.

Statement A means that one class is completely contained in the other. Statement B means that the classes have no members in common. Statements C and D mean that the classes have some, but not all, members in common.

EXAMPLE

No firemen are on the planning commission.

Some politicians are on the planning commission.

Some politicians on the commission are lawyers.

All members of the commission serve two years except lawyers, who serve one-year terms. All politicians on the planning commission who are not lawyers are female.

If all of the above statements are true, which of the following must also be true?

(A)   All politicians on the commission are also lawyers.

(B)   Some of the lawyers on the commission are also firemen.

(C)   Some of the firemen are politicians.

(D)   The politicians on the planning commission all serve one-year terms.

(E)   All female politicians on the planning commission serve two-year terms.

Notice that the question asks you "which of the following *must* be true?" To answer this question you must go through a process of elimination. Choice (A) cannot be true because sentence three of the passage says that SOME of the politicians on the commission are lawyers. This means that not all are lawyers. Choice (B) cannot be true, since sentence one of the passage says that no firemen are on the commission. Some of the firemen may be politicians, (C), but they may not be politicians on the commission. However, there is nothing in the passage that requires any politicians to be firemen, so choice (C) fails. Sentence four of the passage says that all non-lawyers serve two years on the commission. Sentence three says that only some of the politicians on the commission are lawyers, which means that some politicians on the commission are non-lawyers. Therefore, some politicians serve two-year terms, and choice (D) fails. Choice (E) must be true. Since all politicians on the commission who are not lawyers are female, and all non-lawyers on the commission serve two-year terms, all female politicians must serve two-year terms.

Venn Diagrams

The same question can be answered much more easily through the use of a Venn diagram. A Venn diagram is a graphic illustration of claims made in a categorical argument. A Venn diagram consists of circles which represent the classes mentioned in the argument. The examinee can find the answer much more easily by using a Venn diagram than by using the logical process of elimination described above.

Let's look back at the four standard forms of categorical statements. Each can be represented by the use of Venn diagrams.

A. All x are y.

For this kind of statement, draw two circles, one inside the other.

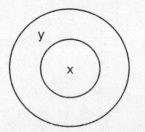

The diagram indicates that all x are contained in y.

B. No x are y.

For this kind of statement, draw two circles that do not overlap one another.

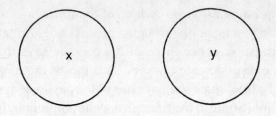

The diagram indicates that the classes x and y are completely separate.

C. Some x are y.

For this type of statement, draw two circles that partly overlap one another.

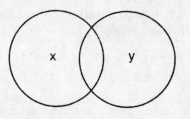

The diagram indicates that the two classes have some members in common.

D. Some x are not y.

Draw the same type of diagram as for C above. The diagram indicates that the two classes have some members in common.

Drill: Common Forms of Deductive Arguments

DIRECTIONS: The questions in this section are based on the reasoning contained in brief statements or passages. For some questions, more than one of the choices could conceivably answer the question. However, you are to choose the **best** answer; that is, the response that most accurately and completely answers the question. You should not make assumptions that are by common-sense standards implausible, superfluous, or incompatible with the passage.

1. No firemen are on the planning commission.

    Some politicians are on the planning commission.

    Some politicians on the commission are lawyers.

    All members of the commission serve two years except lawyers, who serve one-year terms. All politicians on the planning commission who are not lawyers are female.

    If all of the above statements are true, which of the following must also be true?

    (A) All politicians on the commission are also lawyers.

    (B) Some of the lawyers on the commission are also firemen.

    (C) Some of the firemen are politicians.

    (D) The politicians on the planning commission all serve one-year terms.

    (E) All female politicians on the planning commission serve two-year terms.

2. All golfers who are not club members are invited. All doctors are golfers, but there are doctors who are not invited.

   Which of the following conclusions may be derived from the statements above?

   (A) No doctors are invited.

   (B) Some golfers are club members.

   (C) Some doctors are invited.

   (D) No golfers are invited.

   (E) All golfers are doctors.

3. If the statements in the above question are all true, which of the following statements must be FALSE?

   (A) Some who are not golfers are doctors.

   (B) Some doctors are invited.

   (C) If Drew is a doctor, he is not invited.

   (D) Some doctors are club members.

   (E) If Alice is invited, she is not a club member.

4. There are students, as well as faculty, who are active in campus politics. All who are active in campus politics are encouraged to join the University Governing Board.

   If the statements above are true, which of the following must also be true?

   (A) All who are encouraged to join the University Governing Board are active in campus politics.

   (B) All who are encouraged to join the University Governing Board are faculty or students.

   (C) Some who are encouraged to join the University Governing Board are not students or faculty.

(D) Some students are encouraged to join the University Governing Board.

(E) Some students are not encouraged to join the University Governing Board.

5. I love you. Therefore, I am a lover. All the world loves a lover. Therefore, you love me.

In terms of its logical structure, the argument above most closely resembles which of the following?

(A) Adam is a man. Men are homo sapiens. Therefore, Adam is a homo sapien. Homo sapiens are rational. Therefore, Adam is rational.

(B) Sam got to work on time yesterday, the day before, and for the last 50 working days. Therefore, Sam is dependable. Dependable people get raises. Therefore, Sam will get a raise.

(C) I like to talk to Pete. Therefore, I am a patient person. Everyone likes to talk to patient people. Therefore, Pete likes to talk to me.

(D) An orderly universe had to be created by a rational God. The universe is orderly. Therefore, God is rational. A rational God would not allow sin to go unpunished. You sinned. Therefore, you will be punished.

(E) Lifting weights strengthens the body. You lift weights, therefore, you are strong. Strong people are happy. Therefore, you are happy.

Common Forms of Deductive Arguments Detailed Explanations of Answers

1. **(E)**   Categorical Argument Using Venn Diagrams.

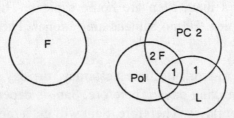

Now, using the Venn diagram, you can answer the question. We see that (A) need not be true, since all of Pol which intersects PC does not also intersect L. (B) need not be true, although it may be true. (C) need not be true, although it may be true. (D) cannot be true, since part of Pol which intersects PC has 2 in it. (E) must be true, since that part of Pol which intersects PC but not L has both F and 2 in it.

2. **(B)**   Categorical Argument. (A) The passage states that there are doctors who are not invited, not that no doctors are invited. There may be doctors who are not club members and are invited. (B) The only golfers who are not invited are club members. All doctors are golfers, and there are doctors who are not invited. Therefore, some of the doctor-golfers are club members. (C) To say that "there are doctors who are not invited" is not to say that some doctors are invited. Perhaps all of the doctors are not invited. (D) One cannot tell if any golfers are invited or not. Perhaps all golfers are club members, in which case none are invited. (E) That all doctors are golfers does not mean that only doctors are golfers.

3. **(A)**   Categorical Argument. If this were true some doctors would not be golfers. The statement is necessarily false, since the second sentence states that all doctors are golfers. (B) We cannot tell from the passage if some doctors are invited or not, so this is not necessarily false. (C) Without knowing if Drew is a club member, we cannot say if he would be invited or not. (D) This statement must be true. Some doctors must be club members, since: all doctors are golfers; some doctors are not invited, and; the only golfers who are not invited are club members. (E) This need not be false. We cannot tell if anyone other than golfers

is invited. If Alice is a golfer she is not a club member. If she is not a golfer, she may or may not be a club member.

4.   **(D)**   Categorical Argument. (A) need not be true. That all who are active in campus politics are encouraged to join does not mean that everyone who is encouraged to join is active in campus politics. Some may not be active, yet be encouraged to join. Choice (B) need not be true. The passage states that all faculty and students who are active in campus politics are encouraged to join. This does not necessarily mean that others, who are not students or faculty, are not encouraged to join. Perhaps administrators or community leaders are also encouraged to join. Choice (C) need not be true. It is possible that only faculty and students are encouraged to join, and no one else. The passage does not specify. Choice (D) must be true. The passage states that there are students active in campus politics, and that all those in that category are encouraged to join. Choice (E) need not be true. It is possible that all students are active in campus politics. Therefore, all students would be encouraged to join.

5.   **(C)**   Categorical Argument. The argument is structured to show that certain feelings which one person has for another must be reciprocated. In other words, the feelings in the first person must produce like feelings in the second person. Choice (C) best parallels that type of reasoning. Only one difference occurs between the passage and choice (C). In the passage, the object of the feelings is being addressed. In answering the object of the feeling was being spoken of in the third person. Choices (A), (D), and (E) employ standard syllogistic reasoning. The syllogism is the method used in deductive reasoning. The syllogism takes the form:

   If A = A
   and B = C
   then A = C.

In choice (A) the argument is:
   Adam = Man;
   Man = Rational;
   therefore Adam = Rational.

Choice (D) uses a slightly different formulation:
   If A then B;
   A, so B.
   If B, then C cannot be present without D.
   B with C, therefore D follows.

In the passage,
   A = orderly universe;
   B = rational God;
   C = sin.

COMMON FORMS OF INDUCTIVE ARGUMENTS

As described in the chart, there are five types of Inductive Arguments: Generalization, Causal Arguments, Circular Reasoning, Ad Hominen Arguments, and Ambiguity.

Generalization

In an inductive generalization, something is said to be characteristic of an entire class of things based on the fact that it is characteristic of certain individuals of that class.

EXAMPLE

> Every tennis player I've played at club X is a server and volleyer. Therefore, most of the tennis players at club X are probably servers and volleyers.

This is an invalid argument and probably not a very strong one. The determining factor here is how many players the author has played relative to the total number of players at club X. If the author has played 45 percent of the players, the conclusion is strengthened. If he has played only five percent, the conclusion is weakened.

For a generalization from members of a class to the whole class to be warranted, the sample must be REPRESENTATIVE of the class. This means that, ideally, the sample must possess all of the relevant features of the class, and in the same proportion. No generalization based on an unrepresentative sample is trustworthy. For that reason, the questions on the test are likely to focus on the representativeness of the sample.

Causal Arguments

A causal argument is one which states that something, Y, caused something else, Z. Causal arguments establish a cause-and-effect relationship between two phenomena. Let's say you ate a green apple. Before you ate it, your stomach felt fine. After you ate it, you had a stomach ache. You reason that eating the apple caused your stomachache, thus you have made a causal argument.

Many passages in logical reasoning involve causal arguments. In causal argument questions you are usually asked to: (a) identify a causal argument, (b) recognize an alternative explanation, or (c) recognize that the argument makes the logical fallacy *post hoc, ergo propter hoc* (in other words, because X follows Y, Y must cause X).

Circular Reasoning

Circular reasoning refers to a type of argument in which the speaker assumes as a premise that which the argument is supposed to prove.

EXAMPLE

> God must exist because the Bible says so, and the Bible is the authoritative word of God.

What we have here is an argument which supposedly proves that God exists based on the authority of the Bible. But the authority of the Bible depends on God's existence. Some proof! A logical reasoning question based on such reasoning might look like this:

God must exist because the Bible says so, and the Bible is the authoritative word of God.

The argument in the passage above makes which of the following errors?

(A) It confuses two different meanings of a word.

(B) It treats a dissimilar event as analogous to the present one.

(C) It assumes what it tries to prove.

(D) It makes a claim by overgeneralizing from specific evidence.

(E) It contains a logical contradiction.

The answer is (C), for the reasons explained above. Choice(A) is incorrect because there is no ambiguity about the meaning of the words in the argument. Since no events per se are discussed, choice(B) is incorrect. Choice(D) may appear plausible at first glance, but does not apply to this case. Overgeneralizaton occurs when an author asserts that A will follow B reapeatedly because A followed B once, or asserts that because one member of a class possesses a certain trait all members of the class possess that trait. Choice(E) is incorrect because there is no logical contradiction in the argument. A logical contradiction occurs when both parts of an argument cannot be true. In the present case, it may be true that both God exists and the Bible is the authoritative word of God.

Ad Hominen Arguments

Ad hominem arguments are arguments that attack the speaker instead of trying to refute his argument. The identity or character of the speaker usually has no influence on the quality of the argument. Saying "Mrs. Brown is ignorant, so her argument that high school students shouldn't be allowed to eat lunch off campus is preposterous" does not refute the argument, it only makes Mrs. Brown mad. Passages which contain ad hominem arguments will usually ask you "The passage above does which of the following?" The answer will be something like "Attacks the person making the argument."

Ambiguity

Some questions will turn on ambiguous use of words or phrases. A word or phrase is ambiguous if it can be assigned more than one meaning and it is not clear from the context which meaning is appropriate.

EXAMPLE

She did nothing well.

This might mean that nothing she did was done well. Or it could mean that she was good at doing nothing. Other examples are:

He was hot.

I know a little German.

I broke his glasses.

Many items on the test which employ ambiguity will offer a verbal exchange between two speakers and then ask you something like: "The disagreement between (person 1) and (person 2) cannot be resolved until _____." The answer will be something like: "Agree on a definition of the word _____ (whichever word is ambiguous).

Drill: Common Forms of Inductive Arguments

DIRECTIONS: The questions in this section are based on the reasoning contained in brief statements or passages. For some questions, more than one of the choices could conceivably answer the question. However, you are to choose the **best** answer; that is, the response that most accurately and completely answers the question. You should not make assumptions that are by common-sense standards implausible, superfluous, or incompatible.

---

1. A survey done last month at Central Mall showed that 89 percent of the shoppers surveyed said they do most of their shopping on the east side of town. Therefore, it is safe to say that if the mall had been placed on the east side of town, rather than in the center of town, merchants in the mall would receive more business.

   The argument above depends on which of the following assumptions?
   I. Business is likely to pick up at Central Mall as the town grows to the west.
   II. The shoppers sampled were representative of all shoppers at Central Mall.
   III. Each of the shoppers surveyed visited several stores in the mall.

   (A) I only   (D) I and II only

   (B) II only   (E) I, II, and III

   (C) III only

2. The price of cotton clothes shot through the roof in June of this year. This year's cotton harvest will likely be one of the worst on record, and this no doubt accounts for the rise in prices.

   The argument in the passage above does which of the following?

(A)   Cites expert opinion to prove a point

(B)   Relies on statistical data to prove a point

(C)   Offers an explanation of a phenomenon

(D)   Criticizes a commonly held opinion

(E)   Argues by analogy

3.   The price of cotton clothes shot through the roof in June of this year. Government projections say this year's cotton harvest will likely be one of the worst on record, and this no doubt accounts for the rise in prices.

Which of the following, if true, would most seriously weaken the conclusion of the argument above?

(A)   Demand for cotton clothes has fallen rapidly since the price increase.

(B)   There was an industry-wide strike in the cotton clothes manufacturing industry in May.

(C)   Most cotton for the clothes industry comes from domestic production.

(D)   Government projections of crop harvests are correct about 70 percent of the time.

(E)   Consumers don't pay as much attention to government projections as manufacturers and retailers do.

4.   Mike: The night before the chemistry final I went out and got drunk. I made an A on the test.

Craig: My physics final is tomorrow. Let's go out and get drunk tonight so I can make an A on my final.

Craig makes which of the following mistakes in the passage above?

(A)   He cites an example to prove a point.

(B)   He assumes that event A caused event B simply because A preceded B.

(C)   He identifies a contradiction in Mike's statement.

(D)   He reiterates his conclusion rather than supplying evidence to support it.

(E)   He misinterprets the meaning of the words "got drunk."

5.   Every time I wash my car, it rains. I just finished washing my car, so it is going to rain.

The argument in the statement above makes which of the following errors?

(A)   It confuses two different meanings of a word.

(B)   It identifies a contradiction.

(C)   It assumes what it tries to prove.

(D)   It makes a claim by overgeneralizing from specific evidence.

(E)   It contains a logical contradiction.

Common Forms of Inductive Arguments Detailed Explanations of Answers

1. **(B)** Generalization. The answer is (B), II only. For the author to draw a valid conclusion from the sample population, that population must be representative of all shoppers at the mall. On the other hand, the survey might have been taken only at the east exit to the mall, in which case most of those surveyed might well be residents of the east part of town who parked on that side of the mall. In that case, it would be logical to expect them to do most of their shopping near their homes on the east side of town. If the author had done the survey at the west exit, many shoppers might have said they do their shopping on the west side of town.

The conclusion of the argument is that business would be better in the mall if it had been placed on the east side of town. This conclusion is based on two assumptions: (a) that the preference of those surveyed to shop on the east side of town represents a general preference of shoppers in the town; (b) that since most people prefer to shop on the east side of town, businesses located there receive more business than those located in the center or on the west side of town. To reach the conclusion it is not necessary to assume that business will pick up as the town grows to the west (assumption possibility I), although that might in fact happen. Nor is it necessary to assume that each shopper surveyed visited several stores in the mall (assumption possibility III). Whether the shoppers surveyed visited one or several stores while in the mall has little or no effect on the conclusion. Therefore, we may eliminate answer choices (A), (C), (D), and (E).

2. **(C)** Causal Argument. The answer is (C), since the author of the passage is making a causal argument to explain the rise in prices. The author does not, (A), cite any expert opinion. Nor are any statistical data offered, (B). Choice (D) is not correct because the author does not refer to any commonly held opinion which he criticizes. Choice (E) is incorrect because there is no attempt by the author to use a similar situation to prove a point in the present case.

3. **(B)** Causal Argument. The answer to the question is (B), because it provides an alternative explanation for the rise in prices. If there was a strike in the manufacturing industry in May, production would have gone down. This would be more likely to drive up the price of cotton clothes in June of this year than would projections of a poor harvest in the fall. Choice (A) is incorrect because demand decreased AFTER the price increase, so it could not be a cause of the price increase; and (b) decreased demand would be more likely to cause a fall rather than a rise in prices. Choice (C) would strengthen the conclusion, not weaken it. If most cotton for clothing comes from domestic production, then projections of a poor harvest would likely have a greater impact on prices than if most cotton for clothes came from foreign production. Choice (D) might weaken the argument somewhat, since government projections are incorrect about 30 percent of the time. Still, a record of being correct 70 percent of the time is pretty good, so the government projection would tend to make manufacturers anticipate a shortage of cotton in the near future. Choice (E) does not weaken the argument, since hiking prices would most likely be a response of manufacturers and retailers to the government projections. If (E) is true, consumers would be more likely to react to the price hikes themselves (perhaps by buying fewer cotton clothes) than to the government projections.

4. **(B)** Ambiguity. The answer is (B). Craig assumes that the reason Mike made an A was because he got drunk, and he makes that assumption on the grounds that getting drunk preceded getting an A. He does not (A) cite any examples to prove a point. He does not (C) identify any contradiction in Mike's statement. He does not (D) reiterate a conclusion. He does not (E) misinterpret the meaning of the words "got drunk."

5. **(D)** Circular Reasoning and Causal Argument. The correct choice is (D) because, although it may actually rain every time the car is washed, the act of washing the car does not provide causality for rain. Just because event A was followed by event B once, does not mean that A will follow B repeatedly. A is not the cause of B. It must occasionally rain when the car *hasn't* been washed, as well as the occasions when the car has been washed. Choice (A) is incorrect because it does not confuse two different meanings of a word. Answer choice (B) is not correct because there is no contradiction presented. Choice (C) is not the correct response, because it does not assume what it is trying to prove. Choice (E) is incorrect because there is no logical contradiction in the argument. A logical contradiction occurs when both parts of an argument cannot be true. It is true that it rains, and it is true that the car gets washed, but these events are mutually exclusive, and can occur without each other.

TIPS FOR FOLLOWING DIRECTIONS

Keep this in mind:

> ➤ Tip 1   Notice that you are instructed to choose the best answer that most accurately and completely answers the questions. In addition, you should not make assumptions that are implausible, superfluous, or incompatible with the passage based on common knowledge.

> ➤ Tip 2   Be sure that the answer you choose answers the question.

TIPS FOR ANSWERING QUESTIONS

Consider these tips:

> ➤ Tip 1   Remember, whenever a study is used to support a claim, an inductive argument is being employed.

> ➤ Tip 2   Look for themes in the first and last sentences of passages. That's where they can usually be found.

> ➤ Tip 3   Use diagramming where it is helpful in understanding the argument and the type of reasoning used.

> ➤ Tip 4   Use the process of elimination to weed out choices.

> ➤ Tip 5   Read the passage carefully for ideas.

> ➤ Tip 6   If the questions following a passage are short, you may want to read them first, so that you know what to look for when reading the passage.

CHAPTER 4

Logical and Critical Reasoning Practice Test

LOGICAL AND CRITICAL REASONING PRACTICE TEST

1. Ⓐ Ⓑ Ⓒ Ⓓ Ⓔ
2. Ⓐ Ⓑ Ⓒ Ⓓ Ⓔ
3. Ⓐ Ⓑ Ⓒ Ⓓ Ⓔ
4. Ⓐ Ⓑ Ⓒ Ⓓ Ⓔ
5. Ⓐ Ⓑ Ⓒ Ⓓ Ⓔ
6. Ⓐ Ⓑ Ⓒ Ⓓ Ⓔ
7. Ⓐ Ⓑ Ⓒ Ⓓ Ⓔ
8. Ⓐ Ⓑ Ⓒ Ⓓ Ⓔ
9. Ⓐ Ⓑ Ⓒ Ⓓ Ⓔ
10. Ⓐ Ⓑ Ⓒ Ⓓ Ⓔ
11. Ⓐ Ⓑ Ⓒ Ⓓ Ⓔ
12. Ⓐ Ⓑ Ⓒ Ⓓ Ⓔ
13. Ⓐ Ⓑ Ⓒ Ⓓ Ⓔ
14. Ⓐ Ⓑ Ⓒ Ⓓ Ⓔ
15. Ⓐ Ⓑ Ⓒ Ⓓ Ⓔ
16. Ⓐ Ⓑ Ⓒ Ⓓ Ⓔ
17. Ⓐ Ⓑ Ⓒ Ⓓ Ⓔ
18. Ⓐ Ⓑ Ⓒ Ⓓ Ⓔ
19. Ⓐ Ⓑ Ⓒ Ⓓ Ⓔ
20. Ⓐ Ⓑ Ⓒ Ⓓ Ⓔ
21. Ⓐ Ⓑ Ⓒ Ⓓ Ⓔ
22. Ⓐ Ⓑ Ⓒ Ⓓ Ⓔ
23. Ⓐ Ⓑ Ⓒ Ⓓ Ⓔ
24. Ⓐ Ⓑ Ⓒ Ⓓ Ⓔ
25. Ⓐ Ⓑ Ⓒ Ⓓ Ⓔ
26. Ⓐ Ⓑ Ⓒ Ⓓ Ⓔ
27. Ⓐ Ⓑ Ⓒ Ⓓ Ⓔ
28. Ⓐ Ⓑ Ⓒ Ⓓ Ⓔ
29. Ⓐ Ⓑ Ⓒ Ⓓ Ⓔ
30. Ⓐ Ⓑ Ⓒ Ⓓ Ⓔ

LOGICAL AND CRITICAL REASONING PRACTICE TEST

> **DIRECTIONS**: The questions in this section are based on the reasoning contained in brief statements or passages. For some questions, more than one of the choices could conceivably answer the question. However, you are to choose the **best** answer; that is, the response that most accurately and completely answers the question. You should not make assumptions that are by common-sense standards implausible, superfluous, or incompatible with the passage.

1. The latest study indicates that women who exercise daily have a higher rate of metabolism than women who do not exercise, lending support to the view that lack of exercise contributes to slow metabolism.

    The argument would be weakened most by pointing out which of the following?

    (A) Statistics can be deceiving.

    (B) Many genetic backgrounds were represented in both the exercising and non-exercising groups.

    (C) Participants in the study were chosen at random from a larger population.

    (D) Some women who did not exercise had higher rates of metabolism than some women who did.

    (E) Many variables, such as the ages and diets of participants, were not accounted for in the study.

2. An advertisement I just heard says that more dentists recommend Doubledent gum for their patients who chew gum. If that is true, Doubledent is preferred by a majority of dentists for their patients who chew gum.

    Which of the following is the strongest objection to the conclusion in the passage?

    (A) Not all dental patients chew gum.

    (B) Dentists should not recommend any brand of gum, since chewing gum may damage expensive dental work.

    (C) Some dentists do not recommend Doubledent gum for their patients who chew gum.

    (D) The phrase "more dentists recommend Doubledent gum for their patients who chew gum" is too ambiguous to provide support for the author's conclusion.

    (E) Dentists are not the best qualified persons to judge which gum their patients should chew.

3. No one under age 35 is a Vietnam veteran. Some Vietnam veterans are on the school board. All members of the school board are under age 50.

    Assuming the above statements to be true, which of the following is/are necessarily true?

    I. Every member of the school board is between the ages of 35 and 50.

    II. Vietnam veterans on the school board are between the ages of 35 and 50.

    III. Some members of the school board are over age 34.

    (A) I only   (D) I and II only

    (B) II only   (E) II and III only

    (C) III only

4. Who is responsible for crime? It is not the criminal. He is just a sick person in need of professional counseling. It is not the victim, who just happens to be in the wrong place at the wrong time. It is not the police, who have been hampered in law enforcement by citizens who refuse to get personally involved in stopping crime. No, you and I are the responsible parties.

    The reasoning of the author of the above passage is most like that of the person who would argue that

    (A) physicians are to blame for illness.

    (B) public apathy is responsible for deaths caused by drunken drivers.

    (C) criminals are responsible for murder.

    (D) foremen are responsible for poor performance by workers.

    (E) companies are responsible for toxic waste.

5. South Korea, a developing country, has a high rate of economic growth. Brazil, a developing country, has a low rate of economic growth. Japan, a developed country, has a high rate of economic growth. The United States, a developed country, has a low rate of economic growth.

    Which of the following most closely expresses the main point of the passage above?

    (A) High economic growth rates can be expected in some developing countries.

    (B) High economic growth rates can be expected in some developed countries.

    (C) High or low economic growth rates cannot be predicted on the basis of whether a country is developing or developed.

    (D) High or low economic growth rates can be predicted by a variety of factors.

    (E) There is no way to predict which countries will have high or low economic growth rates.

6. Barry: My company started out with a 51 percent share of the whitchit market in 1982. My company's sales of whitchits has increased by an average of four percent per year since then. Since there is, and has been, only one other company which sells whitchits, my company is currently the major competitor in the whitchit market.

   Sue: Your company is no longer the major competitor in the whitchit market. Your company currently has only 48 percent of the market, compared to my company's 52 percent.

   Assuming all statistics quoted in the passage to be true, which of the following must necessarily be true?

   I. Overall sales of whitchits has increased since 1982.

   II. Sue's company has increased its sales by more than an average of four percent per year since 1982.

   III. If overall sales by Sue's company declines, overall sales by Barry's company will increase.

   (A) I only

   (B) II only

   (C) III only

   (D) I and II only

   (E) I, II, and III

7. Nobody complains that it is morally wrong for time and weather to cause houses and cars to deteriorate. However, let someone put a dent in another's car or cause damage to another's house, and everyone says that the perpetrator has done an injustice. This shows just how arbitrary we all are in making moral judgments.

   Someone criticizing the conclusion in the passage above would most likely point out that

   (A) morality is always arbitrary, since it depends on arbitrary societal standards.

   (B) the discrepancy is a result of ambiguity in the term "damage."

   (C) weather does not dent cars.

   (D) many people make arbitrary decisions.

   (E) nature is unable to make choices about its actions, while people can.

8. Regardless of what Jim says, baseball is a more refined sport than ice hockey. This is so because more refined people watch baseball rather than ice hockey. You can tell which people are more refined simply by the fact that they prefer the more refined sport to the less refined one.

A logical criticism of the argument above would emphasize that it

(A) establishes a general rule on the basis of one experience.

(B) appeals to questionable authority.

(C) engages in circular reasoning.

(D) attacks a speaker's reputation, rather than addressing his argument.

(E) fails to give exceptions to a general rule.

9. At a district managers' meeting the speaker said: "We have instituted a no smoking policy at our plant to discourage workers from taking breaks." Before the policy went into effect, workers took an average of 1.9 breaks per day. Now that average is down to 1.3.

Which of the following may be inferred from the passage about the way that a worker's wages are determined?

(A) Workers are paid a fixed hourly rate.

(B) Workers are paid according to seniority.

(C) Workers are paid for each unit produced.

(D) Workers are paid on the basis of overall plant production.

(E) Workers are paid for time spent in actual production.

10. Coach: Angie, you are failing to improve at volleyball because you are not practicing your spiking technique.

Angie: Coach, I spend more hours per day at practice than anyone on the team. Last night I was still at practice while everyone else showered.

The major flaw in Angie's response is that she

(A) misunderstands the word "practice."

(B)   avoids the problem by referring to practicing in general, rather than practicing the specific technique.

(C)   disputes the coach's claim by stressing that her spiking technique is fine.

(D)   avoids the problem by stressing what she does best.

(E)   assumes that the coach is overly critical of her.

Questions 11 and 12 refer to the following passage.

Intelligent people always vacation in the Bahamas rather than in Hawaii. One can identify intelligent people by the fact that they have gone to the Bahamas rather than Hawaii.

11.   A logical criticism of the above argument would likely point out that the author

(A)   uses the term "intelligent" in too broad a sense for it to have any meaning.

(B)   generalizes from one example to prove a point about a whole class of people.

(C)   presupposes the very point he is trying to establish.

(D)   assumes that the Bahamas are a better vacation spot than Hawaii.

(E)   fails to prove that the Bahamas are a better vacation spot than Hawaii.

12.   The reasoning in which of the following passages is most like that in the previous passage?

(A)   Homemakers prefer Vizz to Cleansit for their household cleaning chores. Since homemakers are the best judges of home cleaning products, Vizz must be better.

(B)   Homemakers prefer Vizz to Cleansit for their household cleaning chores. Vizz may be used on a variety of surfaces, therefore, it is the best choice.

(C)   Advanced tennis players prefer the new oversized rackets to the standard sized ones. The oversized rackets have more power, which is why advanced players prefer them.

(D) People with class drive Porsches rather than Volkswagens. Porsches usually last longer than Volkswagens.

(E) People with class drive Porsches rather than Volkswagens. You can identify people with class by the fact that they drive Porsches.

13. Assault rifles should not be outlawed. After all, they are just another type of gun, and if one type of gun should be outlawed, why not all of them? But Americans have a long tradition of ownership of guns. Admittedly, assault rifles have few uses other than killing people; but what's at stake here is the American tradition of private ownership of guns.

Assuming each of the following statements is true, which could best be used to counter the author's argument?

(A) Assault rifles can be used for target practice.

(B) The American tradition of gun ownership included the ownership of hunting guns only.

(C) Assault rifles are used in many crimes.

(D) Assault rifles have only recently been developed.

(E) Police forces all around the country are in favor of a ban on the ownership of assault rifles.

14. Eddie: Desmond and Molly's divorce last year is clear evidence of the importance of economic factors in personal relationships. Didn't Desmond also lose his job last year? That's what probably led to the breakup of the marriage.

Brenda: You're wrong, Eddie. Desmond and Molly separated in August. Desmond lost his job in September. What led to the big breakup was Desmond's affair with Lucy in July. It was after she found out about the affair that Molly kicked Desmond out of the house.

Which of the following best describes the weakness in Eddie's claim on which Brenda focuses?

(A) Eddie only considers the economic factors influencing the situation and thus misses some of the other important factors, especially the psychological aspects of the relationship.

(B) It is quite possible that Desmond and Molly will get back together again.

(C) The personal problems leading to the divorce began prior to Desmond's losing his job.

(D) Eddie ignores the many examples of couples who did not get divorced even though the husband or the wife lost his or her job.

(E) Eddie ignores the possibility that Desmond has found a new and even better job.

15. A child, whose parents were hearing impaired and used sign language, could hear normally. Because the child had asthma, he had to stay indoors and was therefore not exposed to normal speakers of language. All of the friends and other visitors to the home were also hearing impaired and communicated to the parents in sign language. The parents kept the television on so that the child could hear language and learn to speak. Although the child learned sign language from his parents, he did not learn to speak and understand spoken language.

Which of the following conclusions can most properly be drawn from the information above?

(A) The language a child learns is determined by innate factors inherited from his parents.

(B) The language used on television is not correct usage.

(C) A young child would not understand the subject matter of television programs.

(D) Interaction is necessary in order to learn a language.

(E) Children do not learn correct usage until they go to school.

16. Since real estate prices are down in the city, this house would probably be a good buy.

Which of the following arguments most closely resembles the one above?

(A) Chicago had a record high temperature of 101° today, so all of Illinois must be hot.

(B)   Since only 67 percent of its graduates found employment last year, a degree from that school is not worth very much.

(C)   Since Conners won last week's tournament, he is likely to win again this week.

(D)   Since dogs are loyal, old Blue should be also.

(E)   Since I hate picnics, I'll just eat at home alone.

17.   Never has a leader of the former Soviet Union looked so weak coming to a summit with an American president. In Moscow, political upstarts to his right and left openly ridicule him. The Baltic states are trying to peel away; as many as four more Soviet republics may follow. After five years of tinkering with the economy, he has fixed too little, too late; but more radical reforms promise inflation and unemployment.

Which of the following is not a premise for the conclusion that the former Soviet Union looks weak?

(A)   The leader is ridiculed by his own people.

(B)   America looks stronger by comparison.

(C)   Baltic republics threaten to peel away from the Soviet Union.

(D)   The economy has not been reformed enough.

(E)   Too much reform would hurt the economy.

18.   There have been many attempts, primarily among theologians, to ascertain the contribution which Whitehead's process philosophy might make to social and political theory. Unfortunately, when one examines this growing body of literature, one becomes aware that a serious study of Whitehead's own social and political thought has been largely neglected. This neglect is no doubt due in part to the fact that Whitehead never produced a systematic political theory. While determination of his political beliefs is difficult, it is necessary if process philosophers and theologians are to assess accurately Whitehead's potential contribution to social and political theory.

Which of the following, if true, would weaken this passage's argument?

(A)   Whitehead's process philosophy has not made a contribution to social and political theory.

(B) A serious study of Whitehead's own social and political thought has been largely neglected.

(C) Whitehead never produced a systematic political theory.

(D) There has been a serious study of Whitehead's social and political thought.

(E) Determination of Whitehead's political beliefs is not difficult.

19. In Leibniz's system, the issue of freedom occupies a prominent position. Moreover, since for him freedom does not only involve absence of external impediments, but also, among other things, the power to will as one should, it directly conflicts with weakness of will. Consequently, his views on weakness of will are to be regarded as relatively central to the system. Furthermore, systematic considerations aside, the issue of weakness of will is of considerable intrinsic interest because of its theoretical and practical aspects alike.

Of the following, which is not a premise offered as support for the conclusion that Leibniz's views on the weakness of will are central to his system?

(A) Freedom involves absence of external impediments.

(B) Weakness of will involves absence of external impediments.

(C) Freedom directly conflicts with weakness of will.

(D) The issue of freedom is important to Leibniz's system.

(E) Freedom involves the power to will as one should.

20. Lacrosse is an amateur sport in which successful players do not follow collegiate careers with high paying professional contracts. Also most existing intercollegiate lacrosse programs either do not produce revenue or do not produce sufficient revenue to cover their operating costs. As a result, many college and university athletic administrators assign lacrosse a low priority. At the same time this situation has had the favorable consequence that lacrosse has been largely free of NCAA violations and the controversies concerning the academic progress of student athletes.

Which of the following conclusions is consistent with the writer's assertions?

(A) Lacrosse generates high revenues for colleges.

(B)   Lacrosse has forced many NCAA violations.

(C)   Lacrosse has remained consistent with traditional values of intercollegiate sport as a valuable extracurricular experience for serious students.

(D)   Since lacrosse has many successful players, it receives strong support from college and university athletic administrators.

(E)   Good lacrosse players in college often receive high paying professional contracts.

21.   Robert: Striking by employees is counterproductive; while the strike goes on, the plant is effectively shut down, and the corporation loses money. This means that the employees themselves lose in the long run.

      Leah: I disagree. Sometimes striking is necessary to get the attention of management. If the plant loses a little money, the management will be forced into making concessions they otherwise wouldn't.

The misunderstanding between Robert and Leah is based on

(A)   different definitions of the word "strike."

(B)   differing evaluations of the interests of the management.

(C)   a disagreement over what is in the employees' long-term interest.

(D)   different social agendas.

(E)   different views on the need for negotiation.

22.   Everyone knows that correlations do not establish causal relationships among the variables they measure. And yet the examples of precisely such relationships being inferred are too numerous to require documentation. It has become commonplace, for example, to conclude that, because a given group of rich or successful men with few exceptions had rich or successful parents, the achievements of the sons were due to the good things conferred on them by their fathers. Perhaps they were. Unfortunately, the aggregate data are unrevealing.

Which example would add support to the conclusion of this argument?

(A)   A woman born of wealthy parents who has succeeded because of good things conferred on her by her father

(B)   A poor and unsuccessful women who has rich parents

(C)   A group of rich or successful women who had rich or successful parents

(D)   Rich fathers who conferred good things on their daughters

(E)   A woman born of wealthy parents who has made a success of herself without help from her parents

23.   A study published by a noted scholar says that desire for territorial acquisition is the leading cause of war. I disagree. Most wars are the result of ideological differences between the leadership of the warring countries. From the Peloponnesian War between aristocratic Sparta and democratic Athens, to WW II between the fascist Axis and democratic Allies, ideology has been at the root of most human conflict.

Which of the following best describes the form of the argument above?

(A)   It argues from analogy.

(B)   It offers an alternative explanation.

(C)   It attempts to discredit the noted scholar's study by challenging its methodology.

(D)   It attacks the credibility of the noted scholar.

(E)   It cites evidence that the scholar overlooked.

24.   The road crew includes both men and boys. All men are hateful and all boys are insubordinate. Every insubordinate person is hateful, so every person on the crew is hateful.

Which of the following is an assumption that would make the conclusion in the argument above logically correct?

I.   There are no women or girls on the road crew.

II.   Being hateful is the same as being insubordinate.

III.   No member of the road crew is insubordinate.

(A)   I only   (D)   I and II only

(B)   II only   (E)   II and III only

(C)   III only

25. The second proposition is this: an action done from duty has its moral worth, not in the purpose that is to be attained by it, but in the maxim according to which the action is determined. The moral worth depends, therefore, not on the realization of the object of the action, but merely on the principle of volition according to which, without regard to any objects of the faculty of desire, the action has been done.

Which of the following actions could not have moral worth, according to this argument?

(A) An action done by someone who wants to do what is right, regardless of the consequences

(B) An action done by someone who is concerned about the maxim according to which the action is determined

(C) An action done with evil intentions that has good consequences

(D) An action done out of appropriate volition

(E) An action done without regard to the objects of the faculty of desire

26. *Driver's News* rated our newest sports coupe number one for performance and road-handling. Come test drive the Rocket turbo and see for yourself!

This advertisement would lead logically to the conclusion that you should consider buying the car if you already held which of the following assumptions?

(A) *Driver's News* is a reliable, informed, and objective source of information about automobiles.

(B) Buying an expensive car is a good investment since it will last longer than a cheaper car.

(C) Most people buy a car for its style, not for its durability.

(D) The best buy is the car that gets the most miles per gallon.

(E) Other people will tend to judge your character according to the kind of car that you drive.

27. Fifty volunteers from local churches operate a soup kitchen in Sawyer's Falls, a city of 100,000. The volunteers have found that the number of individuals showing up for free soup varies in proportion to the unemployment rate. At the moment, unemployment is at five percent and 350 people show up every day. The soup kitchen is funded through donations from local churches. Recent inflation has increased the cost of food, but the volunteers are asking for increased donations so that they cannot only maintain the present program but offer a complete meal — not just soup.

    Which of the following changes in these factors would help the volunteers to carry out their plan?

    (A) An increase in unemployment from five percent to six percent

    (B) An increase in inflation from four percent to five percent

    (C) A decrease in the donations

    (D) An increase in the number of volunteers from 50 to 100

    (E) A decrease in unemployment from five percent to four percent

28. Mark said, "I always lie."
    Jay said, "I always tell the truth."
    Kevin said, "Mark always lies."
    Jeannie said, "Jay always lies."

    Which ones could you believe?

    (A) Both Jay and Mark, but neither Jeannie nor Kevin

    (B) Both Mark and Kevin, but neither Jay nor Jeannie

    (C) Jay, but not Mark, Jeannie, or Kevin

    (D) Either Jay or Kevin, but neither Mark nor Jeannie

    (E) Either Jay or Jeannie, but neither Mark nor Kevin

Questions 29 and 30 are based on the following.

Due to an oil embargo, the price of heating oil in the United States soared. In order to cut heating costs, some people invested in insulation for their homes. Then, as a result of new exploration and increased conservation, the price of oil went back down again.

29. Which of the following can be inferred from the passage?

   (A) The government should give a tax credit for insulation and other energy-saving improvements.

   (B) As a result of new sources of oil and decreased demand, there was no longer a shortage of supply.

   (C) The government should stockpile oil in case of a military emergency.

   (D) The government should subsidize solar energy.

   (E) Nuclear power is the only alternative to dependence on foreign sources of energy.

30. Given the lower price of oil, some homeowners concluded that the money spent on insulation was not a good investment; this conclusion, however, is probably unwarranted because it can be inferred from the passage that

   (A) the price of oil may rise again.

   (B) sooner or later we will deplete all of the earth's oil supply.

   (C) without such conservation measures the price would not have come back down.

   (D) the oil producing countries cannot stick together in enforcing an embargo.

   (E) nuclear energy is not a safe alternative.

PRACTICE TEST

1. (E)	7. (E)	13. (B)	19. (B)	25. (C)
2. (D)	8. (C)	14. (C)	20. (C)	26. (A)
3. (E)	9. (A)	15. (D)	21. (C)	27. (E)
4. (B)	10. (B)	16. (D)	22. (E)	28. (E)
5. (C)	11. (C)	17. (B)	23. (B)	29. (B)
6. (D)	12. (E)	18. (D)	24. (A)	30. (C)

Logical and Critical Reasoning
Detailed Explanations
of Answers

1. **(E)** Choice (A) is a generalized statement that tells us nothing about any misuse of statistics in this particular study. Choice (B) would strengthen the study, since it would control one variable, genetic background. In other words, if all members of one group were from the same genetic background and all members of the other group were from another background, it could be true that differences in genetic background account for differences in metabolic rate, and exercise had little or no effect on metabolic rate. Choice (C) would strengthen the results of the study. By choosing participants at random, we help ensure that they are representative of the general population. Choice (D) is the most attractive alternative to (E). However, some variation would not affect the value of the study. No generalization from a study such as this need be true in every case to be valid. Choice (E) is the best answer. Failure to control variables is one of the major problems in studies such as this. By not controlling for variables such as diet and age, the study might have overlooked alternative explanations for differences in metabolic rates.

2. **(D)** Choice (A) fails because the passage itself implies that some patients do not chew gum. The conclusion is that Doubledent is preferred by dentists for patients who DO chew gum. Choice (B) is certainly an objection to the conclusion in the passage, but not the strongest one. The dentists are not said to recommend that everyone chew gum, only that those who already chew gum should use a certain brand. The implication is that if the patient must chew gum, he or she should chew the brand least likely to do damage. By saying that "more dentists recommend Doubledent," the passage implies that not all do. Choice (C), then, tells us nothing that is not apparent in the passage. Choice (D) is the best answer. By saying "more dentists recommend Doubledent gum..." the ad tells us very little. The statement could mean that more recommend it now than before, although the number may have only gone from a single dentist recommending it to two. The statement could mean that more recommend it than another brand, although it is still next to the last in number of recommendations. Since ascertaining the exact meaning is impossible, the phrase is too ambiguous to be useful in forming conclusions. Choice (E) is probably not a true statement. If dentists are not qualified to make judgments about which gum is best for their patients, who is?

3.   **(E)**   This is an example of categorical reasoning, for which you can use a Venn diagram. Draw one circle for Vietnam veterans. Label it VV and put in it 35+. Draw another circle which partially overlaps VV. Label it SB and put in it 50–. In the section of the two circles which overlaps, put 35+ and 50–. Now test statements I–III against the diagram. Statement I cannot be true, since the only thing we know about all members of SB is that they are under 50 (50–). Some may be under 35. II is true, since the overlapping part of VV and SB are 35 or older (35+) and under 50 (50–). III is true, since some Vietnam veterans are on the school board (the overlapping part of the circles), and they are 35 or older. The answer, then, is (E).

4.   **(B)**   The author does not blame the perpetrator (the criminal), the victim (the one who suffers from the act), or the police (those responsible for stopping the perpetrator). Instead, he blames the public for apathetically refusing to get involved. Choice (A) is incorrect because the physician is analogous to the police. Choice (B) is the best answer because it blames public apathy, not the one immediately responsible for the act. Choice (C) is incorrect because it blames those immediately responsible, whereas the author of the passage does not. Choice (D) is incorrect because the foremen, who are analogous to the police in the passage, are blamed. Choice (E) is incorrect because companies would be analogous to the criminals in the passage.

5.   **(C)**   While the passage gives some support for both (A) and (B), neither is the main point. If the author wished to make either point, there would be no need for a discussion of countries with low growth rates. Choice (C) is the best answer. It takes into account the discussion of countries with high and low growth rates and countries which are developed and developing. The main point of the passage is that both developed and developing countries may have either high or low growth rates. There is no way, based on the variables "developing or developed," to predict which countries will have high and which will have low growth rates. Choice (D) fails because the passage says nothing about which factors might be helpful in making such a prediction. Choice (E) fails because the passage does not consider and dismiss other factors which might aid such a prediction.

6.   **(D)**   Statement I must be true. The only companies selling whitchits are Barry's and Sue's. If Barry's company has sold more whitchits each year since 1982, but has lost market share, the total amount of whitchits sold must have increased since 1982. Statement II must be true. If Barry's company had the largest market share in 1982, and has increased its sales by four percent per year since then, it follows that Sue's company has increased its sales by more than an average of four percent per year since 1982. If Sue's company had not increased its sales by more than an average of four percent per year, her company could not

have overtaken and passed Barry's company as the leader in whitchit sales. Statement III need not be true. A 10 percent decline in sales by Sue's company might correspond to a 10 percent decline in total sales of whitchits. Sales by Barry's company might remain exactly the same even if sales by Sue's company decline.

7.   **(E)**   The clear difference between weather and human action is (E), that humans can make choices about what they do, whereas nature cannot. For that reason, we hold humans but not nature responsible for actions. Choice (A) does not get to the root of the problem, which is that where there is no choice, no moral judgment can be made. Choice (B) is incorrect because the meaning of "damage" is clear enough for the purposes of the passage. Choice (C) is incorrect, since denting a car is only one type of damage the author could have mentioned as an example. Choice (D) fails for the same reason as (A), that weather cannot be measured by moral standards.

8.   **(C)**   The problem with the passage is that it presupposes what it is trying to prove, namely that baseball is more refined than ice hockey. We know baseball is more refined based on the premise that people who watch it are more refined. But we know they are more refined because they watch it. So we have this problem: our premise, that more refined people watch baseball, depends on our conclusion, that baseball is more refined. The truth of our premise depends on the truth of our conclusion. Choice (A) is out, since no particular experience is cited from which a general rule is drawn. There is no appeal to authority, (B). Choice (D) receives some scant support from the reference to Jim, but Jim's reputation is not attacked. (E) is incorrect.

9.   **(A)**   The speaker says that the ban on smoking was meant to discourage breaks. Therefore, breaks must cost the plant money. The most obvious way for this to be true is if the worker is paid by the hour, (A). Then, if a worker was on a break, he or she would still be getting paid, even though not producing. This would cost the plant money. Seniority, (B), is incorrect. If the workers were paid for each unit produced, (C), they would not be getting paid for time spent on breaks. If they were paid on overall plant production, (D), breaks would not necessarily cost the plant money. If they were paid only for time spent in production, (E), breaks would not necessarily cost the plant money.

10. **(B)**   There is no reason to believe that (A) Angie does not understand the word "practice." She does (B) avoid the problem by referring to practice in general, rather than practicing the specific technique. She does not (C) dispute the coach's claim about her technique, only that she does not practice enough in general. She does not (D) stress what she does best. Nor does she necessarily

assume that the coach is overly critical of her (E), only that he is mistaken this time.

11. **(C)** This is an example of circular reasoning. The author argues that intelligent people choose one thing over another, and that act of choosing, by itself, makes them more intelligent. Look for the answer which duplicates this type of argument. (A) The word "intelligent" has at least this meaning in the passage: intelligence is something that enables one to make better choices. Therefore, (A) cannot be the answer, because it states that the term does not have any meaning. (B) The only thing that could be construed as an example is the choosing of one vacation spot over another. However, the passage cites no evidence to show that that choice is an intelligent one. Therefore, this example cannot establish the point that they are more intelligent for having made it. (C) This is exactly what the passage does. (D) and (E) are both plausible answers. However, they do not get the major flaw of the argument, which is circular reasoning.

12. **(E)** You are seeking an argument which asserts something as a fact, then attempts to prove it by asserting it again in a slightly altered form. (A) This is a valid form of the syllogism. It takes the following form: Homemakers prefer Vizz; homemakers are the best judges of home products; therefore, Vizz must be better. (B) This offers two reasons why Vizz is better: Homemakers prefer it; and it is useful in more than one type of chore. (C) This offers two reasons to show why oversized rackets are preferable: advanced players — who should be good judges of rackets — prefer them; and they have more power. (D) This tells you two things about Porsches: people with class like them; and they last longer. (E) This attempts to establish that Porsches are better by arguing that people with class drive them. But the only way you know that those people have class is that they drive Porsches. This is identical to the reasoning in the passages.

13. **(B)** The best way to counter an argument is to show that one of the author's premises is untrue. This destroys the argument from within, without having to prove the conclusion false. The choice which takes this approach is (B). The author of the passage states twice that ownership of assault rifles should be protected because ownership of guns is part of an American tradition. He admits that assault rifles have no use for hunting. But if the American tradition of gun ownership applies only to hunting weapons, it offers no support for the protection of assault rifles. The major premise of his argument is destroyed. (A) That assault rifles can be used for target practice neither adds nor detracts from the argument. The author of the passage said that they have few uses other than killing people. Target practice happens to be one of those other uses. Since it is unobjectionable in itself, it would not convince a proponent of assault rifles to be against them;

nor would it convince an opponent to be in favor of them. (C) This is a plausible objection to the ownership of assault rifles. However, it does not, in and of itself, destroy the basis of the author's argument, which is that the American tradition supports gun ownership. (D) This is somewhat beside the point. They are still guns, and the author's argument is not weakened. One could argue that the tradition of gun ownership had not been meant to include such weapons, but that is the argument which is made more directly by (B). (E) This is a plausible objection to the argument. However, the author could probably point to groups around the country which favor his position. Logically speaking, an appeal to authority is not as effective for undermining an argument as disproving its premise.

14. **(C)** Eddie presents an argument of cause and effect. He claims that the loss of employment caused the divorce. The weakness that Brenda focuses on is the chronology of the events. Brenda argues that the loss of employment did not cause the divorce because the separation leading to the divorce preceded the loss of employment. Thus, the correct answer is (C): "The personal problems leading to the divorce began prior to Desmond's losing his job."

The other choices do not correctly identify "the weakness...on which Brenda focuses." Choice (A), for example, identifies a possible weakness in Eddie's argument, that he only considers economic factors. This is not, however, the weakness that Brenda chooses to attack. Similarly, choice (D) implies that Eddie, in order to draw general conclusions about economic factors influencing personal relationships, ought to consider more than just one example. That would be a valid criticism, but again, it is not the weakness on which Brenda focuses. The relevance of choices (B) and (E) is less clear. There is nothing in the given information to suggest that Desmond and Molly either will or will not get back together again. Similarly, there is nothing to suggest that Desmond either has or has not found a new and better job. Even if they did get back together again, or even if he did find a new and better job, it is not learned from the context how this would affect Eddie's argument. His argument could still be valid. The divorce might have been caused by economic factors even if they did get back together again or even if Desmond found a new and better job. The point is that neither issue is part of Brenda's criticism.

15. **(D)** Since the child learned sign language from his parents, but did not learn spoken language from the television, the conclusion to be drawn would be based on the apparent difference between the two sources: parents and television. If (A) were true, it would follow that you would learn the language of your parents and not the language of a TV set. It does not follow, however, that (A) is necessarily true. Since he has not been isolated from his parents by, for example, adoption,

there is no evidence that he inherited sign language rather than learning sign language from watching his parents and communicating with them. Although we might consider the possibility of innate factors, the information gives us no evidence one way or the other. Choices (B) and (E) are irrelevant since the evidence involves the acquisition of any language at all, not the learning of correct usage. There is no evidence from the passage to support the notion that the language on television is particularly correct or incorrect. There is no evidence from the passage to support the notion that correct usage can only be learned at school. Whether correct language is heard on television or whether it is only learned at school are topics that have no bearing on this case because this child did not speak *any* language, correct or incorrect. Although (C) offers a plausible explanation, it is not supported by the evidence one way or the other. We do not know from the evidence whether or not the child could understand the subject matter. Finally, the answer is (D) because it is the most obvious difference between the two sources. The child probably interacted with his parents on a daily basis. With regard to the television he could be, at best, only a passive receiver of language. Apparently, this was not enough. Thus, the conclusion that "can most properly be drawn" is that "Interaction is necessary in order to learn a language."

16. **(D)** The passage reasons from the general to the particular. One class of things, real estate in this city, is down in price; therefore, a member of this class, this particular house, must be a good buy (down in price). Eliminate (A) because it reasons from the particular to the general: from Chicago to the state where it is located. (B) uses a fact about graduates of a school to form a judgment about that school. The graduates are not the general class of things of which this school is a member. (C) argues that something is likely to happen because it has happened before. One might choose (E) thinking that picnics is a class of things, and the speaker is making the following argument: since I hate all picnics, I would hate the one today. However, one cannot tell if the speaker means that he will stay home from today's picnic (one member of the class); or from all future picnics (the entire class). (D) is exactly like the passage. Dogs is the class, old Blue the particular member of the class.

17. **(B)** The writer supports the conclusion with three premises: the leader is ridiculed by political adversaries at home (A); Baltic republics threaten to peel away (C); and the economy has not been reformed enough (D), although too much reform would also hurt the economy (E). The writer never claims that America looks stronger by comparison, thus (B) is not one of the premises.

18. **(D)** The argument concludes that there should be serious study of Whitehead's thought because many scholars believe this thought has contributed to social and political theory, but no one has studied Whitehead's thought itself

(B). If there has been such a study (D), then the argument is incorrect and, hence, weakened. Whether or not Whitehead's philosophy has actually made any contribution (A) is irrelevant to the premise that scholars *believe* it has and that they should therefore try to support their beliefs. It is also irrelevant to this belief whether determination of Whitehead's political thought is difficult (E) and whether he produced a systematic political theory (C).

19. **(B)** The premises are as follows: Freedom (of will) is important to Leibniz's system (D). For him, freedom, but *not* weakness of will (B), involves absence of external impediments (A) and the power to will as one should (E), and freedom conflicts with weakness of will (C).

20. **(C)** The writer explicitly denies that lacrosse generates high revenues (A), has forced many NCAA violations (B), receives strong support from athletic administrators (D), or leads to high paying professional contracts for its players (E). So these statements would all be inconsistent with the writer's assertions. However, if the writer's assertions are true, it is quite possible that lacrosse has remained consistent with traditional values of intercollegiate sports. Hence, choice (C) is consistent.

21. **(C)** Both speakers agree that the word "strike" means a work stoppage, so eliminate (A). The interests of management are not discussed, so eliminate (B). While the speakers may have different social agendas (D), this is not clear from the passage, since they both appear to be concerned with the long-term interests of the workers. Eliminate (E) since negotiation is not discussed. The argument obviously centers on what is in the long-term interests of the workers; more specifically whether they will benefit in the long run from a strike. The answer, then, is (C).

22. **(E)** The conclusion is that many people *incorrectly* infer that correlations establish causal relationships among the variables they measure. The writer notes and rejects any belief in any necessary causal connection between a group of rich or successful men and the men's rich or successful parents: just because both child and parents are rich and successful, does not mean the parents' wealth or success caused the child's wealth or success.

A woman whose success was caused by her father's gifts (A), would show that a causal connection is possible and thus would weaken the argument. A poor and unsuccessful woman who has rich parents (B) would not exemplify the correlation in question and thus would be irrelevant to the argument. A group of rich or successful women with rich or successful parents (C), and rich fathers who confer good things on their daughters (D), exemplify the correlation in question, but the examples do not make any assertion about a causal connection. Thus, the examples neither weaken the argument nor support the conclusion.

A woman who was successful without help from her wealthy parents (E), would be evidence that a correlation is possible without a causal connection and thus would support the passage's conclusion.

23. **(B)** The author does not argue from analogy, (A), but cites two wars as examples which support his interpretation (B). Webster's *Collegiate Thesaurus* gives the following definition of analogy: "...expression involving explicit or implicit comparison of things basically unlike but with some striking similarities...." (G. and C. Merriam Co: Springfield, Mass., 1976). An analogy, then, is based on the similarity of certain attributes of two things, when the things themselves are essentially different. One war is not essentially different from another, as an athletic contest is from a war. One war would not, then, normally serve as an analogy for another. The author does not (C) try to discredit the scholar's methodology. In fact, nothing is said about the methodology of the study. It may rely heavily on statistical techniques, or it may be a survey of previous accounts of war. We are not told which. The author does not say that the scholar should be disbelieved because he is not trustworthy (D). We cannot tell from the passage if the scholar overlooked the wars cited by the author of the passage. Perhaps he did not, but rather gave a different interpretation of what caused them.

24. **(A)** Assumption I is necessary to make the conclusion correct, since one cannot assume on the basis of the first sentence that the road crew contains ONLY men and boys. Assumption II is not necessary to the conclusion, since the passage establishes that everyone on the crew who is insubordinate is also hateful. It is not necessary, then, for the purposes of the conclusion, that insubordination and hatefulness be synonymous. Assumption III contradicts one of the premises of the argument, so it is not a possibility. The correct answer, then, is (A).

25. **(C)** The point of this passage is that the maxim (guiding principle) behind an action, not the consequences of an action, determine whether or not the action is morally good. In other words, only if an action is done with good intentions is it a good act. Thus, an action done with evil intentions, but good consequences (C) would still be bad. An action done by someone who wants to do what is right could be good, regardless of the consequences (A). An action done by someone who is concerned about the maxim of it (B) could be good, provided the maxim were good. An action done out of appropriate volition (good will) (D) would be good. And an action done without regard to desirable objects or consequences (E) could be good.

26. **(A)** A logical argument must follow from assumptions. The argument is valid if it is logical in form, that is, if the conclusions would follow from those assumptions. The assumptions may be granted for the sake of argument, but frequently as in this case the argument is based on a tacit assumption, something assumed but not explicitly stated. The problem is to figure out which of the five statements provides a premise for the argument that would lead, if true, to the desired conclusion. The rating of the automobile by *Driver's News* leads to the conclusion that the automobile is worth buying only if the consumer believes that *Driver's News* is a reliable source of information. The other four statements may or may not also be true. They do not necessarily contradict the argument, but neither are they necessary for it. If the car in question is expensive, then (B) for example would lead you to buy it. The advertisement does not say, however, whether the car is relatively expensive or not. Choice (C) is about consumer preference. This might influence the design and sale of cars, but it is not a necessary assumption for the consumer. Choice (D) would be important if mileage were an issue. Since the advertisement does not discuss mileage, statement (D) is not relevant. The advertisement does not specify a type of character associated with the car, so choice (E) is not a necessary assumption for the argument. Thus, each statement must be examined as a part of a logical argument. Only (A) provides a premise from which the advertisement leads to the conclusion.

27. **(E)** The problem here is to sort out the various factors and determine how each one will affect the outcome. The ability of the volunteers to provide for the needy is determined by the income that the center receives and the costs that the center incurs. If the volunteers are going to provide more, they must either increase the income or lower the costs or both. An increase in unemployment (A) would result, according to the problem, in an increase in costs since there would be more people showing up for soup. An increase in inflation (B) would result in an increase in costs, since it would further increase the cost of buying food. A decrease in donations (C) would decrease the income and, therefore, limit what the volunteers could provide. An increase in the number of volunteers (D) would have no effect since they are not contributing money and they are not paid. Of the five factors listed, only (E) would enable the volunteers to provide more food to each person requesting it. The decrease in unemployment would, according to the problem, result in a decrease in the number of people showing up. This would lower the costs, and with lower total costs the volunteers would be able to provide each person with more food.

28. **(E)** Jay claims that he always tells the truth. It may or may not be so, but we *could* believe it because it might be so. Jeannie claims that Jay always lies. Again this may or may not be so. Each one could be right, but they cannot both

be right. We *could* believe either one, but not both. If Jay is right, then Jeannie is not right. If Jeannie is right, then Jay is not right.

What Mark says cannot be true because it implies a contradiction. If it were true, then he would not be lying about always lying. In that case, however, we would have to assume that he was lying and it was not true. Thus, what Mark claims cannot be true. Since it cannot be true that Mark *always* lies, what Kevin claims cannot be true. So it follows that we could believe neither Mark nor Kevin.

Thus, the correct answer is (E) "Either Jay or Jeannie, but neither Mark nor Kevin."

29. **(B)** The key to solving this kind of problem lies in the final words of the question: "...can be inferred from the passage." Among the various possible answers there may be statements that are true, statements that one could agree with, statements even that are *consistent* with the given information. They do not, however, follow from that given information. The problem, then, is to find the one statement that is logically implied by the given information. In this case the answer is (B) because an increase in exploration and conservation resulting in a lower price implies an increase in supply. The other choices are all statements of policy. With these statements one might reasonably agree or disagree, but the statements are not directly implied by the information given. Many other factors may be relevant to these issues. A tax credit for conservation (A), a strategic stockpile of oil (C), a subsidy for solar energy (D), and a reliance on nuclear energy (E) are complex issues. These issues are certainly related to the information given, but the information given does not in and of itself imply a particular position on these issues one way or the other.

30. **(C)** Basic to the solving of this problem is the recognition that the conservation measures themselves have contributed to the reduction in price. Of course, an individual might argue that he or she could save money by not insulating and letting everyone else insulate. Since the total amount of insulating would still be about the same, the net effect on the price of oil would still be about the same. It would not work, however, if everyone took that approach. Then, in the absence of conservation, the price would not go down. The other answers may or may not be true, but in any case they cannot be inferred from the passage. Nothing in the passage implies that (A) "the price of oil may rise back up again." As for (B), we may assume that the oil supply is finite, but this is not implied by the passage. Likewise, (D) and (E) are statements that one might or might not agree with, but that cannot be inferred from the passage. Whether or not the oil producing countries can maintain a unified policy is not implied by the passage. Whether or not nuclear energy is a safe alternative is not implied by the passage.

CHAPTER 5

Analytical Reasoning Diagnostic Test

ANALYTICAL REASONING
DIAGNOSTIC TEST

1. Ⓐ Ⓑ Ⓒ Ⓓ Ⓔ
2. Ⓐ Ⓑ Ⓒ Ⓓ Ⓔ
3. Ⓐ Ⓑ Ⓒ Ⓓ Ⓔ
4. Ⓐ Ⓑ Ⓒ Ⓓ Ⓔ
5. Ⓐ Ⓑ Ⓒ Ⓓ Ⓔ
6. Ⓐ Ⓑ Ⓒ Ⓓ Ⓔ
7. Ⓐ Ⓑ Ⓒ Ⓓ Ⓔ
8. Ⓐ Ⓑ Ⓒ Ⓓ Ⓔ
9. Ⓐ Ⓑ Ⓒ Ⓓ Ⓔ
10. Ⓐ Ⓑ Ⓒ Ⓓ Ⓔ
11. Ⓐ Ⓑ Ⓒ Ⓓ Ⓔ
12. Ⓐ Ⓑ Ⓒ Ⓓ Ⓔ
13. Ⓐ Ⓑ Ⓒ Ⓓ Ⓔ
14. Ⓐ Ⓑ Ⓒ Ⓓ Ⓔ
15. Ⓐ Ⓑ Ⓒ Ⓓ Ⓔ
16. Ⓐ Ⓑ Ⓒ Ⓓ Ⓔ
17. Ⓐ Ⓑ Ⓒ Ⓓ Ⓔ
18. Ⓐ Ⓑ Ⓒ Ⓓ Ⓔ
19. Ⓐ Ⓑ Ⓒ Ⓓ Ⓔ
20. Ⓐ Ⓑ Ⓒ Ⓓ Ⓔ
21. Ⓐ Ⓑ Ⓒ Ⓓ Ⓔ
22. Ⓐ Ⓑ Ⓒ Ⓓ Ⓔ
23. Ⓐ Ⓑ Ⓒ Ⓓ Ⓔ
24. Ⓐ Ⓑ Ⓒ Ⓓ Ⓔ
25. Ⓐ Ⓑ Ⓒ Ⓓ Ⓔ
26. Ⓐ Ⓑ Ⓒ Ⓓ Ⓔ
27. Ⓐ Ⓑ Ⓒ Ⓓ Ⓔ
28. Ⓐ Ⓑ Ⓒ Ⓓ Ⓔ
29. Ⓐ Ⓑ Ⓒ Ⓓ Ⓔ
30. Ⓐ Ⓑ Ⓒ Ⓓ Ⓔ

Analytical Reasoning
Diagnostic Test

    This diagnostic test is designed to help you determine your strengths and your weaknesses in analytical reasoning. The diagnostic test is set up in the same format that appears on many standardized tests. It contains all of the various question types which you are likely to encounter while taking these exams. By taking this diagnostic test, you will be able to determine which question types pose the most difficulty for you. It is wise to study all the material contained within the reviews, but by taking this diagnostic test, you will be able to determine the areas in which you are the weakest, and concentrate on those particular question types.

> **These types of questions are found on the following tests:**
> **GRE and LSAT**

Diagnostic Test

> **DIRECTIONS**: Each group of questions in this section is based on a set of conditions. In answering some of the questions, it may be useful to draw a rough diagram. Choose the response that most accurately and completely answers each question.

Questions 1 – 4 refer to the following statements.

The state of Texana contains six cities.

F is the westernmost city and south of K.

J and K are south of I.

G and J are west and south of K and south of F.

H is east of I and south of J.

I is east of K.

1. The northernmost city in Texana is

    (A) G.   (D) J.

    (B) H.   (E) K.

    (C) I.

2. The easternmost city in Texana is

    (A) G.   (D) J.

    (B) H.   (E) K.

    (C) I.

3. The southernmost city in Texana is

    (A) G.   (D) H.

    (B) I.   (E) K.

    (C) J.

4. If the above information is true, all of the following statements EX-
    CEPT which must also be true?

    (A) G is west of I.   (D) G is east of J.

    (B) F is south and west of I.   (E) J is west of H.

    (C) H is south and east of K.

Questions 5 – 10 refer to the following passage.

A landscaping crew will plant ornamental trees, shade trees, evergreen trees, ornamental shrubs, evergreen shrubs, and ornamental grasses on a bare housing site. Planting must be done in five consecutive working days, Monday through Friday, and must conform to all of the following conditions:

All evergreens must be planted on the same day.

Ornamentals and evergreens cannot be planted on the same day.

Shade trees must be planted at least one day before evergreen trees.

Ornamental grasses and ornamental trees must be planted on the same day.

Evergreen shrubs must be planted at least one day before ornamental trees.

5.   Which of the following can be planted on the same day?

(A)   Evergreen trees and ornamental shrubs

(B)   Ornamental shrubs and evergreen shrubs

(C)   Shade trees and evergreen shrubs

(D)   Shade trees and ornamental grasses

(E)   Ornamental grasses and evergreen trees

6.   Which of following is an acceptable order of planting, from first to last?

(A)   Shade trees, evergreen shrubs, ornamental grasses

(B)   Shade trees, ornamental grasses, evergreen trees

(C)   Shade trees, ornamental trees, evergreen trees

(D)   Evergreen shrubs, shade trees, evergreen trees

(E)   Evergreen shrubs, ornamental grasses, shade trees

7.   If the crew plants ornamental grasses on Thursday, it CANNOT plant

(A)   evergreen shrubs on Wednesday.

(B)   shade trees on Tuesday.

(C) evergreen trees on Friday.

(D) ornamental shrubs on Friday.

(E) ornamental shrubs on Wednesday.

8. If the crew plants evergreen shrubs on Wednesday, it can plant

(A) ornamental shrubs on Wednesday.

(B) evergreen trees on Friday.

(C) ornamental trees on Tuesday.

(D) shade trees on Monday.

(E) ornamental grasses on Monday.

9. If the crew plants ornamental trees on Friday and shade trees on Tuesday, it can plant evergreen shrubs on

(A) Monday, Tuesday, Wednesday, or Thursday only.

(B) Wednesday or Thursday only.

(C) Tuesday or Thursday only.

(D) Wednesday only.

(E) Thursday only.

10. On how many days can the crew plant ornamental shrubs if it plants shade trees on Monday, evergreen shrubs on Wednesday, and ornamental grasses on Friday?

(A) One   (D) Four

(B) Two   (E) Five

(C) Three

Questions 11 – 14 refer to the following information.

S, T, U, V, W, X, Y, and Z weighed in and then competed in a jumping event.

S weighed more than V and jumped higher than W.

Z weighed less than X and more than W, and did not jump as high as Y.

T weighed more than U and less than W, and jumped higher than Y but not as high as U.

U weighed more than S and did not jump as high as W.

11. Which of the following weighed the least?

    (A) S   (D) V

    (B) T   (E) Z

    (C) U

12. Which of the following jumped the highest?

    (A) T   (D) Y

    (B) U   (E) Z

    (C) W

13. Which of the following statements must be true?

    (A) V weighed less than T and jumped higher than Y.

    (B) T weighed more than Z and jumped higher than Z.

    (C) U weighed more than V and jumped higher than S.

    (D) Y weighed more than Z and jumped higher than Z.

    (E) W weighed more than S and jumped higher than T.

14. Which of the following statements could be true?

    (A) X weighed the most and jumped the highest of the contestants.

    (B) W was third heaviest and jumped fifth highest of the contestants.

(C)   Heavy competitors always jumped higher than lighter ones.

(D)   Lighter competitors always jumped higher than heavier ones.

(E)   T was the sixth heaviest and jumped fifth highest of the contestants.

Question 15 – 18 refer to the following information.

A state dinner will include a rectangular table for seven that presents several seating problems. The guests are three governors (F, G, H), two senators (J, K), and two congressmen (L, M). three guests will sit on one side of the table, three directly opposite on the other side, and one at the head of the table. No one will sit at the foot of the table.

Congressmen cannot be seated next to each other.

Senators cannot be seated directly opposite each other.

Governor F cannot be seated next to Senator J.

Governor G must sit immediately on Congressman L's right.

A governor must sit at the head of the table.

15.   If H sits at the head of the table, G and J sit immediately to his left and right respectively, and L sits next to K, which guest must sit directly opposite Congressman L?

(A)   F   (D)   L

(B)   G   (E)   M

(C)   J

16.   If F sits directly opposite L and between K and M, which guest must sit directly opposite M?

(A)   G   (D)   K

(B)   H   (E)   L

(C)   J

17. If G sits at the head of the table, and F in the middle seat on one side of the table and immediately on K's left, the guest seated directly opposite F must be

(A) G.

(B) H.

(C) J.

(D) L.

(E) M.

18. Which of the following is an acceptable seating arrangement starting with one side at the foot of the table, moving toward the head of the table, and continuing around to the opposite foot of the table?

(A) J, K, L, F, M, G, H

(B) F, M, L, G, H, K, L

(C) M, J, H, G, L, K, F

(D) J, K, F, H, L, G, M

(E) H, M, J, L, G, F, K

Questions 19 – 22 refer to the following statements.

The tenure and promotion boards must be staffed by eight professors — G, H, I, J, K, L, M, and N. There are two boards of three professors each — one board makes tenure decisions and the other makes promotion decisions.

No professor may serve on both boards in the same year.

At least two members of the tenure board must be tenured. The tenured professors, in descending order of seniority, are M, G, N, and J.

At least two members of the promotion board must be full professors. The full professors, in descending order of seniority, are I, H, K, and L.

Each board must have one professor from each of three disciplinary groups —the humanities, the social sciences, and the natural sciences. The humanities professors are G and K; the social sciences professors are H, M, and N; and the natural sciences professors are I, J, and L.

The chair of the tenure board must be the most senior tenured professor among the three board members; the chair of the promotion board must be the most senior full professor among the board members.

19. Which of the following could be the promotion board?

(A) J, L, M

(B) G, I, L

(C)   I, K, L

(D)   G, H, L

(E)   H, K, N

20.   The two boards must include which of the two following professors?

(A)   M and I

(B)   M and K

(C)   I and G

(D)   H and I

(E)   G and K

21.   If N is the chair of the tenure board, the other two members of the tenure board must be

(A)   J and K.

(B)   K and L.

(C)   H and J.

(D)   G and J.

(E)   G and M.

22.   If the tenure board consists of G, N, and I, and if H is too ill to serve on either board, which professor must be chair of the promotion board?

(A)   I

(B)   J

(C)   K

(D)   L

(E)   M

Questions 23 – 25 refer to the following passage.

A dachshund, beagle, bassett, and chow win the top four prizes in the dog show. Their owners are Mr. Kramer, Mr. Tyler, Mr. Hamilton, and Mr. Perry. The dogs' names are Toby, Rusty, Deuce, and Ace. The owners' and dogs' names are not necessarily in any order.

Mr. Hamilton's dog wins neither first nor second prize.

The bassett wins first prize.

Ace wins second prize.

The dachshund is Toby.

Mr. Tyler's dog, the chow, wins fourth prize.

Mr. Perry's dog is Rusty.

23. First prize is won by

    (A) Mr. Kramer's dog.   (D) Toby.

    (B) Mr. Perry's dog.   (E) Deuce.

    (C) Ace.

24. Mr. Hamilton's dog

    (A) is the bassett.   (D) wins second prize.

    (B) is the beagle.   (E) is Rusty.

    (C) is the dachshund.

25. Deuce

    (A) is owned by Mr. Tyler.

    (B) is owned by Mr. Kramer.

    (C) is the beagle.

    (D) is the bassett.

    (E) wins third prize.

Questions 26 – 29 refer to the following statements.

A is older than B and taller than C.

D is younger than E, older than C, and shorter than F.

G is older than H, younger than C, shorter than H, and taller than F.

H is older than A and shorter than C.

26. Which of the following is the youngest?

    (A) A   (D) D

    (B) B   (E) E

    (C) C

27. Which of the following is the tallest?

    (A) A   (D) D

    (B) H   (E) C

    (C) F

28. Which of the following is true?

    (A) A is the second oldest and is the third tallest.

    (B) C is younger than D and taller than H.

    (C) D is the oldest and shortest.

    (D) G is older than E and shorter than A.

    (E) H is older than B and taller than A.

29. Which statement about the group A, B, C, D, E, F, G, and H is necessarily false?

    (A) D is the shortest of the group.

    (B) C is the second tallest of the group.

    (C) D is the second oldest of the group.

    (D) A is the tallest of the group.

    (E) F is the third oldest of the group.

Question 30 refers to the following passage.

Two women, Debbie and Joy, and two men, Al and Jeff, are doctors. One is a dentist, one a surgeon, one an optometrist, and one a general practitioner. They are seated around a square table with one person on each side.

1) Al is across from the dentist.

2) Jeff is not across from the surgeon.

3) The optometrist is on Debbie's left.

4) Joy is the general practitioner.

5) The surgeon and general practitioner are married to each other.

6) The general practitioner is not on Joy's left.

7) The general practitioner is across from the optometrist.

30. Which statement is repeated information?

(A) 1   (D) 7

(B) 5   (E) None of these

(C) 6

ANALYTICAL REASONING
DIAGNOSTIC TEST

1. (C)	7. (C)	13. (E)	19. (D)	25. (A)
2. (B)	8. (D)	14. (A)	20. (E)	26. (B)
3. (B)	9. (B)	15. (E)	21. (A)	27. (A)
4. (D)	10. (D)	16. (C)	22. (C)	28. (B)
5. (D)	11. (D)	17. (C)	23. (B)	29. (E)
6. (A)	12. (C)	18. (D)	24. (C)	30. (C)

Diagnostic Test
Detailed Explanations
of Answers

1. **(C)** See number 4.

2. **(B)** See number 4.

3. **(B)** See number 4.

4. **(D)** The information provided enables us to draw a map that yields the following information. From north to south, the cities are I, K, F, G/J, H; from west to east, the cities are F, G/J, K, I, H. All cities can be located in relation to each other except G and J, but we know that both are east of F, west of K, north of H, and south of F. Hence, the correct answers to questions 1 – 4 are, respectively, (C), (B), (B), and (D).

5. **(D)** (D) is correct since planting shade trees and ornamental grasses on the same day does not violate any of the planting conditions. (A), (B), and (E) are incorrect because they violate the condition specifying that ornamentals and evergreens cannot be planted on the same day. (C) is incorrect because it violates the conditions that result when the first and third conditions are combined; shade trees must be planted at least one day before all evergreens (condition three specifies evergreen *trees*, but condition one asserts that evergreen shrubs and evergreen trees must be planted on the same day; hence, shade trees must be planted at least one day before evergreen shrubs as well as evergreen trees).

6. **(A)** Only (A) does not violate any of the planting conditions. (B) violates the fifth condition (evergreen shrubs at least one day before ornamental trees) when that condition is combined with condition one (all evergreens on the same day) and condition four (ornamental grasses and ornamental trees on the same day). (C) violates condition five when it is combined with condition one. (D) violates condition three (shade trees at least one day before evergreen trees) when that condition is combined with condition one (all evergreens on the same day); evergreen shrubs cannot be planted before shade trees if evergreen trees are planted after shade trees. (E) also violates condition three when it is combined with condition one.

7. **(C)**   The crew cannot plant evergreen trees on Friday if it plants ornamental grasses on Thursday because ornamental grasses and ornamental trees must be planted on the same day (Thursday), evergreen shrubs must be planted at least one day before ornamental trees (Wednesday or earlier in the week), and all evergreens, including trees, must be planted on the same day (Wednesday or earlier). Hence, evergreen trees cannot be planted on Friday if ornamental grasses are planted on Thursday. None of the other choices – (A), (B), (D), or (E) – violates planting conditions.

8. **(D)**   The crew can plant shade trees on Monday without violating planting conditions (D). (A) violates condition two. (B) violates condition one. (C) violates condition five. (E) violates condition five when it is combined with condition four.

9. **(B)**   Evergreen shrubs cannot be planted on Monday or Tuesday if shade trees are planted on Tuesday because shade trees must be planted at least one day before evergreen trees, and all evergreens must be planted on the same day. Planting evergreen shrubs on Wednesday and Thursday does not violate any planting conditions. Hence, (B) is correct.

10. **(D)**   Only Wednesday is ruled out (ornamentals and evergreens cannot be planted on the same day). Planting the other four days does not violate any planting conditions. Hence (D) is correct.

11. **(D)**   See number 12.

12. **(C)**   The relationship can be clarified by drawing two diagrams. Weight, from heaviest to lightest: X, Z, W, T, U, S, V. Jumping height, from highest to lowest: S, W, U, T, Y, Z. Hence, the answer to 11 is (D) and the answer to 12 is (C).

13. **(E)**   The answer is (E) since we know with certainty that W weighed more than S and jumped higher than T. (A) is incorrect because we do not know how high V jumped. (B) is incorrect because we know T weighed less than Z. (C) is incorrect because we know S jumped higher than U. (D) is incorrect because we do not know how high Y jumped.

14. **(A)**   (A) could be true. We know that X weighed more than the other contestants whose weight we know; X might weigh more than those whose weights we do not know. We do not know how high X jumped; X might have jumped higher than all of the others. (B) cannot be true. We lack information about the jumping heights of two contestants; even if both jumped higher than W,

W can finish no lower than fourth. (C) and (D) are incorrect; as the diagrams indicate, some heavy contestants jumped higher than lighter ones and some lighter contestants jumped higher than heavier ones. (E) cannot be true. We lack information about the weight of one contestant; even if that contestant weighs more than T, T cannot be more than fifth heaviest.

15. **(E)** Remembering that L always sits on G's left, one side of the table is G (opposite J), L, K. This leaves only M and F. However, F cannot be directly opposite L because that would place F next to J, a violation of condition three. Hence, the correct answer is (E).

16. **(C)** One side of the table is K, F, M; F is opposite L, who is on G's left. Therefore, H (the only remaining governor) must sit at the head of the table. K and M must sit opposite G and J, but J cannot sit directly opposite K since both are senators. Hence, J must sit opposite M, so the correct choice is (C).

17. **(C)** If G sits at the head of the table, L is at his left. F and K must be on the opposite side of the table (F cannot otherwise be on K's left), with K farther from the head of the table. J cannot sit directly opposite L since that would place J next to F, nor can J sit directly opposite K since both are senators. Hence, J must sit directly opposite F. The answer is (C).

18. **(D)** Only (D) violates none of the conditions. (A) violates condition four (G on L's right). (B) violates condition one (L and M are next to each other). (C) violates conditions two (J and K are directly opposite each other) and four. (E) violates condition five (L is not a governor).

19. **(D)** (D) meets all of the conditions. Two members are full professors (H), (L); one is from the humanities (G), one is from the social sciences (H), and one is from the natural sciences (L). (A) is incorrect because only one is a full professor; (B) and (C) are incorrect because there is no social sciences representative; and (E) is incorrect because there is no natural sciences representative.

20. **(E)** Since there are two boards, and each board must include a humanities professor, and since there are only two humanities professors, and since professors cannot serve on more than one board, both humanities professors, (G) and (K) must be included. The answer is (E).

21. **(A)** The chair of the tenure board is the most senior tenured member of the board. If N is the chair, then the other tenured member on the board must be J, since he is the only other tenured professor with less seniority than N. The other representative must be from the humanities since N is from the social sciences

and J is from the natural sciences. The humanities representative must be K; it cannot be G, since we know that no tenured professor with more seniority than N can be on the board if N is chairing it.

22. **(C)**   Only K, L, M, and J are left as possible chairs of the promotion board. Neither M nor J can be chair because neither is a full professor. Of the two full professors, K is senior to L; hence, K must be chair of the promotion board.

Questions 23 – 25

A four by four grid listing prizes, breeds, owner, and dog names is needed.

Prize	Breed	Owner	Name
1	bassett	Perry	Rusty
2	beagle	Kramer	Ace
3	dachshund	Hamilton	Toby
4	chow	Tyler	Deuce

23. **(B)**   Once statement (six) identifies the fourth prize winner and you determine that Mr. Hamilton's dog therefore won third prize, it follows that since Ace won second prize, Mr. Perry's Rusty was the bassett that won first prize.

24. **(C)**   The same reasoning process used in question 20 makes Mr. Hamilton's dog the dachshund that won third prize.

25. **(A)**   This can be read from the diagram.

Questions 26 – 29

Let us arrange the letters in two separate categories. The first category will be for age—older and younger. The second category will be for height—taller and shorter.

We represent older with the mathematical "greater than" sign >. We represent taller with a double mathematical "greater than" sign >>.

From the first statement (A is older than B and taller than C), we get this representation:

$$A > B \text{ and } A >> C$$

The second statement (D is younger than E, older than C, and shorter than F) translates mathematically as:

$$E > D > C \text{ and } F \gg D$$

The third statement (G is older than H, younger than C, shorter than H, and taller than F) gives us:

$$C > G > H \text{ and } H \gg G \gg F$$

The fourth statement (H is older than A and shorter than C) gives us:

$$H > A \text{ and } C \gg H$$

Thus, consolidating, we have:

$A > B$		$A \gg C$
$E > D > C$		$F \gg D$
$C > G > H$	and	$H \gg G \gg F$
$H > A$		$C \gg H$

Again, with the mathematical inequality sign we can further consolidate the above in two separate inequality statements:

$$E > D > C > G > H > A > B$$

and

$$A \gg C \gg H \gg G \gg F \gg D$$

26. **(B)** Since $E > D > C > G > H > A > B$, B must be the youngest of the group because it is the least of all the given letters.

27. **(A)** $A \gg C \gg H \gg G \gg F \gg D$. Therefore, A must be the tallest because it is the greatest of all the given letters.

28. **(B)** From the final mathematical representation above, we can see that D > C and C >> H, thus indicating that C is younger than D and taller than H.

29. **(E)** (Note that the correct choice must be a false choice). We see that the only choices that deal with younger-older people are choices (C) and (E). Choice (C) is a true statement, so it is incorrect. Now let us go to the shorter-taller choices — that is, choices (A), (B), and (D). Choice (A) is a true statement, so it is an incorrect choice. Choice (B) is a true statement, so it is an incorrect choice. Choice (D) is a true statement, so it is an incorrect choice. As for choice (E), we cannot determine whether F is the third oldest of the group because F is not included in the younger-older mathematical representation. However, since the other four choices are incorrect, we can, by a process of elimination, conclude that choice (E) is the only correct choice.

Question 30

From statement 1, place Al across from the dentist.

Al

Dentist

(Al is now obviously not the dentist.)

From statement 7, you could tentatively place the general practitioner and the optometrist.

Al

Optometrist (?)   General Practitioner (?)

Dentist

Statement 4 tells you that Joy is the general practitioner. Now you can deduce that Al must be the surgeon, and since Jeff is not across from the surgeon (statement 2), then Jeff must be the optometrist.

The final placement can be made from statement 3, because Debbie must be the dentist, and optometrist (Jeff) must be on Debbie's left.

Al
Surgeon

Jeff   Joy
Optometrist   General Practitioner

Debbie
Dentist

30. **(C)** Statement 4 says that Joy is the general practitioner; therefore, you already knew that the general practitioner could not be on Joy's left (statement 6).

CHAPTER 6

Analytical Reasoning Review

ANALYTICAL
REASONING REVIEW

Analytical Reasoning Questions

Analytical reasoning questions are designed to test your deductive reasoning skills. Such skills, briefly put, enable you to examine evidence provided by an author and arrive at conclusions that follow from such evidence. Deductive reasoning, if it is done correctly and if the evidence given is true, leads you to conclusions that are true and follow with certainty from the evidence. Analytical reasoning questions consist of a set of related statements followed by questions which require the process of deduction based on the set of given statements. The questions do not require knowledge of formal logic or mathematics, although they require knowledge of vocabulary and simple computational ability. They test your ability to analyze given relationships of time, space, grouping, cause and effect, etc., and to draw conclusions from these relationships.

EXAMPLE

Betty, Eva, and Maria were planning on going to a party together. However, the day before the party, two of the women had an argument, such that the following conditions resulted:

CONDITIONS/CLUES

1. If Betty went, then Maria did not go.

2. Eva went only if Betty went.

3. If Maria went, then either Betty or Eva did not go.

4. Maria went to the party.

QUESTION

1. How many of these young women went to the party?

   (A) All three of them   (B) Two of them

(C)   One of them

Note what occurs in this example. You are given a set of conditions (clues) that you are to take as true, and from those conditions (clues) you are to identify the conclusion that follows from them. The question that you must ask yourself is "Which of the three choices follows with necessity from the conditions (clues) given?" And that is the question that you will have to ask yourself throughout this section of the GRE and the LSAT. But now for the solution to this example.

SOLUTION

Clue #4 told us that Maria went to the party. Since Clue #1 told us that if Betty went to the party, then Maria would *not* go, we know immediately that Betty did not go since Maria went. So Betty did not go to the party. And since Betty did not go to the party, we also know that Eva did not go, since Clue #2 told us that Eva would go only if Betty went. As you can see, these conclusions follow with certainty from the conditions given. And so you can conclude that only one of the women went to the party, and that was Maria. The correct answer is (C).

Note that in solving this problem it was not necessary to use Clue #3. Also note that to solve this problem you had to read the conditions/clues carefully in order to determine what conclusions followed from the conditions.

QUESTION TYPES

There are six basic types of deductive reasoning questions that often appear on analytical reasoning tests. Each type is distinguished by the type of relationship expressed in the evidence or the conditions given to you:

1. Attribute Assignment Questions

2. Conditional Relationship Questions

3. Familial Relationship Questions

4. Ordering Relationship Questions

5. Spatial Relationship Questions

6. Time Assignment Relationship Questions

TYPE 1: Attribute Assignment Questions

In this type of question you will be given a group of people or objects, a list of attributes, and a set of conditions, and you will have to determine who or what has which attribute.

EXAMPLE

Albert, Bob, Charlie, Dirk, Edgar, and Frank are going to a play-off game in a distant city and have rented an eight-passenger van for the trip. One of the men always wears a red hat, another is nearsighted, one dislikes Frank, one wears a toupee, one is Charlie's son, and one is diabetic.

CONDITIONS/CLUES

1. The man who is wearing the toupee is the driver, and he is sitting next to Frank, who is sitting directly in front of Charlie's son.

2. Edgar is sitting next to the man who always wears a red hat.

3. Albert is sitting in the center seat of the second row.

4. The man who dislikes Frank is the only person sitting in the last row of the seats in the van.

5. The man who is nearsighted is seated behind Dirk.

6. Edgar is seated to Albert's right.

QUESTION

1.   The person who always wears a red hat is

   (A)   Albert.   (D)   Dirk.

   (B)   Bob.   (E)   Edgar.

   (C)   Charlie.

SOLUTION

Let us call the men A, B, C, D, E, and F, and let us call the attributes r, n, f, t, c, and d, in order to make it quicker and easier to solve the problem.

The first step you should take in answering any question on the GRE and LSAT is to **read the question carefully and determine what type of relationship(s) is/are expressed in both the passage and the list of conditions**. In this passage you are given a list of names, in this case men who are going to a play-off game, and a list of characteristics. In the conditions, you are given clues as to who has what characteristic. And the question asks you to determine who has a specific characteristic, in this case, who always wears the red hat. This, then, is an attribute assignment question.

When you come across such a question, the next step you can take is to use a chart, diagram, or both to keep track of the conditions, and although you don't have to do this, the chart/diagram method has saved time for many students. Because some of the conditions in the problem refer to the seating arrangement in the van, this question could also be considered a spatial relationship problem. It is often the case with analytical reasoning questions that you will find the different types of questions mixed in one problem. We will use both a chart to keep track of the attributes and a diagram to record their seating arrangement. You know that there are six men and six characteristics. One possible chart is the following:

	r	n	f	t	c	d
A						
B						
C						
D						
E						
F						

Remember:

A = Albert   r = red hat
B = Bob   n = nearsighted
C = Charlie   f = dislikes Frank
D = Dirk   t = toupee
E = Edgar   c = Charlie's son
F = Frank   d = diabetic

You should fill in the spaces with "X"s or "O"s, based on the information given in the condition statements—X means "is not," and O means "is." You know that they rented an eight-passenger van. Reading through each condition/clue, we can construct a diagram of the seating arrangement in the van in the following way:

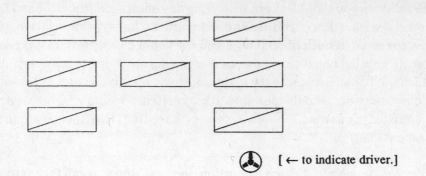

[← to indicate driver.]

Since you will be inserting two pieces of information, the person's name and his attribute, the squares are split in half to make it easier to see what information you still need.

CONDITION/CLUE #1

The man who is wearing the toupee is the driver, and he is sitting next to Frank, who is sitting directly in front of Charlie's son.

Now you should ask yourself what conclusions follow from this condition/clue, and you can use the chart and diagram to keep track of these conclusions.

CONCLUSIONS

1. Frank is NOT the man wearing the toupee, since he is sitting next to the man who is wearing it (the driver).

2. Frank is NOT Charlie's son, since Frank is sitting directly in front of Charlie's son.

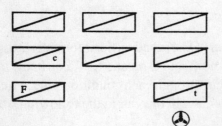

	r	n	f	t	c	d
A						
B						
C						
D						
E						
F				X	X	

CONDITION/CLUE #2

Edgar is sitting next to the man who always wears a red hat.

CONCLUSION

Edgar is NOT the man who always wears a red hat.

	r	n	f	t	c	d
A						
B						
C						
D						
E	X					
F				X	X	

CONDITION/CLUE #3

Albert is sitting in the center seat of the second row.

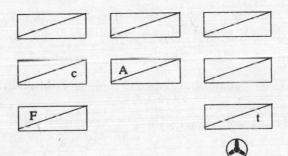

CONCLUSIONS

1. Albert is NOT Charlie's son, since he is not sitting directly behind Frank.

2. Albert is NOT wearing the toupee, since he is not in the driver's seat.

We now show this on the chart:

	r	n	f	t	c	d
A				X	X	
B						
C						
D						
E	X					
F				X	X	

CONDITION/CLUE #4

The person who dislikes Frank is the only person sitting in the last row of seats in the van.

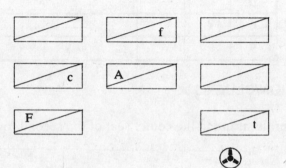

CONCLUSIONS

1. Frank is NOT the person who dislikes Frank, since he is sitting up front.

2. Albert does NOT dislike Frank since he is not in the last row of seats in the van.

	r	n	f	t	c	d
A			X	X	X	
B						
C						
D						
E	X					
F			X	X	X	

CONDITION/CLUE #5

The man who is nearsighted is seated behind Dirk.

CONCLUSIONS

1. Dirk is NOT nearsighted.

2. The person who is nearsighted is NOT sitting in the last row of seats in the van, since Clue #4 told us that the only person seated there was the one who dislikes Frank. From this and from our diagram:

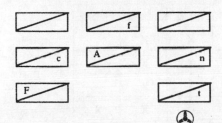

	r	n	f	t	c	d
A			X	X	X	
B						
C						
D		X				
E	X					
F			X	X	X	

it follows that

3. the person who is nearsighted is seated directly behind the driver; and therefore

4. the driver is Dirk; and therefore

5. Dirk is wearing the toupee.

We can also conclude that neither Albert nor Frank are nearsighted, because of the seating arrangement determined thus far.

	r	n	f	t	c	d
A		X	X	X	X	
B				X		
C				X		
D	X	X	X	O	X	X
E	X			X		
F			X	X	X	

CONDITION/CLUE #6

Edgar is seated to Albert's right.

CONCLUSIONS

1. Edgar is Charlie's son.

2. Edgar is NOT nearsighted.

3. Edgar does NOT dislike Frank.

	r	n	f	t	c	d
A		X	X	X	X	
B				X	X	
C				X	X	
D	X	X	X	O	X	X
E	X	X	X	X	O	X
F		X	X	X	X	

Looking at the above chart, we now know that:

1. Albert is NOT Charlie's son;

2. Albert does NOT dislike Frank;

3. Albert is NOT wearing the toupee;

4. Albert is not nearsighted; and

5. since Edgar, who is Charlie's son, is seated to Albert's right and next to the man who always wears a read hat, then we can also conclude that Albert is the man who always wears the red hat.

The correct answer is (A) Albert. Looking at the finished diagram and chart we can see that:

	r	n	f	t	c	d
A	O	X	X	X	X	X
B	X			X	X	X
C	X			X	X	X
D	X	X	X	O	X	X
E	X	X	X	X	O	X
F	X	X	X	X	X	O

1. Frank is the diabetic;

2. Dirk wears the toupee;

3. Edgar is Charlie's son;

4. either Bob or Charlie (but not both) is nearsighted; and

5. either Bob or Charlie (but not both) dislikes Frank.

Again, this example demonstrates how you will be given conditions/clues, and from those conditions/clues you will have to determine what conclusions follow from them.

In summary, you should approach attribute assignment questions using the following method.

1. Read the passage carefully and determine what relationship is expressed in the passage and conditions.

2. Read through each clue and determine what conclusions follow.

3. Keep track of the conclusions via either a diagram or a chart or both.

4. Do not impose your own assumptions/beliefs on the conditions/clues, but rather take them as they are given to you. The importance of this will be made clearer when we get to familial relationship questions.

Drill: Attribute Assignment

DIRECTIONS: Each group of questions in this section is based on a set of conditions. In answering some of the questions, it may be useful to draw a rough diagram. Choose the response that most accurately and completely answers each question.

1. Mr. and Mrs. Johnson and Dr. and Mrs. Steinmiller each have different tastes in music. One prefers rock and roll, one easy listening, one classical, and the last country music. Of the four, only two have brown hair and one of these likes easy listening best. The wife with brown hair likes country music and her husband likes classical music best. Mrs. Steinmiller has blond hair.

    What color hair does Dr. Steinmiller have and what music does he prefer?

    (A) Brown hair and easy listening music

    (B) Brown hair and classical music

    (C) Blond hair and country music

    (D) Blond hair and classical music

    (E) Blond hair and easy listening music

2. The seven members of the Quality Control Division, Mr. Rodriguez, Ms. Unger, Ms. Queen, Mr. Singer, Mr. Thomas, Ms. Winters, and Ms. Vellars, are going to have a group photograph taken, and they will be arranged in a line according to height.

    Ms. Queen is taller than Mr. Thomas.

    Ms. Winters is shorter than Ms. Queen.

    Mr. Rodriguez is taller than Mr. Singer.

    Ms. Vellars is shorter than Ms. Winters.

Mr. Singer is taller than Ms. Winters.

Ms. Unger is taller than Ms. Queen.

If there are two individuals taller than Mr. Rodriguez, who is the second tallest?

(A)   Mr. Singer   (D)   Ms. Queen

(B)   Mr. Thomas   (E)   Ms. Winters

(C)   Ms. Unger

3.   In the Classics Corner of the auto show, the Avanti, Bugatti, Cord, Dusenberg, and Edsel line up. Each has a special ornament: a hood statue, a monogrammed door, a chromed spare-tire cover, a rhodium-plated engine, or eel-skin upholstery. Their order from left to right meets the following conditions:

The Cord is immediately left of the car with the chromed spare-tire cover and immediately right of the car with the rhodium-plated engine.

The Bugatti is immediately left of the car with the monogrammed door.

The only car next to the Avanti is the one with the hood statue.

The car with the monogrammed door is immediately to the left of the one with the eel-skin upholstery.

There are exactly two cars between the Avanti and the Dusenberg.

Which car must have the monogrammed door?

(A)   Avanti   (D)   Dusenberg

(B)   Bugatti   (E)   Edsel

(C)   Cord

4.   A husband and wife hired an architect to design a new house for them. They wanted a master bedroom, a smaller bedroom, a kitchen, a living room, a dining room, and a utility room. The architect designed a rectangular house two rooms wide and three rooms deep. Each room was painted a different color. The colors were red, blue, white, beige, brown, and yellow.

Conditions:

1. The yellow room is at the front of the house on the left. On the right front is the master bedroom, and directly behind it is the red room.

2. The dining room is to the right of the brown room.

3. The small bedroom is at the back of the house.

4. The kitchen, which is not blue or yellow, is in front of and to the left of the utility room.

What color is the dining room?

(A) Yellow   (D) Beige

(B) Red   (E) White

(C) Brown

5. Three couples—A and B, C and D, and E and F—meet at a lecture on ethnicity. B, D, and F are women; the other three are men. Each person has one and only one of the following ethnic origins: African-American, Native American, Swedish, Norwegian, and Italian. (Note that Swedish and Norwegian are both considered Scandinavian.) The following conditions apply:

1. The two people in each couple are not of the same ethnic origin.

2. None of the men is of the same ethnic origin as any of the other men.

3. D is Swedish.

4. Neither A nor E is Scandinavian.

5. F is Native American.

Which of the following statements must be true?

(A) One of the men is Swedish or Italian.

(B) Two of the women are Norwegian.

(C) None of the men is Scandinavian.

(D) Exactly one of the women is Scandinavian.

(E) One of the men is African-American or Italian.

Attribute Assignment
Detailed Explanations
of Answers

1. **(A)** is the correct answer. Because this question asks "what," we know that the situation is one in which the arrangement is stable or fixed. The setup includes three items of information sorted out about four people. In addition, there is the auxiliary relationship in that there are two couples. You can present the information in one chart.

Name	Mr. J	Mrs. J	Dr. S	Mrs. S
Music	Classical	Country		
Hair		Brown		Blond

Now consider the last information.

Name	Mr. J	Mrs. J	Dr. S	Mrs. S
Music	Classical	Country	Easy Listening	Rock and Roll
Hair	Not Brown	Brown	Brown	Blond

Therefore, the answer is (A), Dr. Steinmiller has brown hair and likes easy listening music.

2. **(D)** Because this is a linear ordering problem, we must begin by collecting all the data at our disposal. Remember, "taller than" and "shorter than" are transitive relations— if x is taller than y and y is taller than z, you can derive that x is taller than z. In this problem, certain features of the ordering are guaranteed. The following sequences cannot be violated, although there can be additional letters between the members of these sequences:

  U—Q—T

  U—Q—W

  R—S—W—V

taller   shorter

We must place R in the third spot and begin experimenting with possible combinations. All of the acceptable solutions begin U—Q—R—x—x—x. Thus, Q is the second tallest, and (D) is the correct answer.

3.   **(D)**   is the correct answer. The initial information is summed up as

eCc
Bd
|Ah or hA|
du
A—D or D—A

(Capital letters for the car names, lowercase for the ornaments: c = chromed spare-tire cover, d = monogrammed door, e = rhodium-plated engine, h = hood statue, u = eel-skin upholstery.)

Collecting these together gives
eCc
Bdu
|Ah—D or D—hA|

Placing that on a single diagram gives

1	2	3	4	5
	A̶	A̶	A̶	
E̶				E̶
D̶		D̶		D̶
			B̶	B̶
c̶	c̶		c̶	c̶
u̶	u̶			
d				d̶
h		h		h
e	C	c		
			D	
A	h	B	d	u
				E

The negative entries come from the impossibility of fitting one or another of the lists into the space with the denied item in that space. The first line comes from the Avanti being at one end or the other. The second is from the fact that there is a car on either side of the Cord. The third is from the fact that the Dusenberg is fourth from one end or the other. The fourth from the fact that there are two cars right of the Bugatti. And so on. When all of the negative entries have been made, it appears that only the car with the rhodium-plated engine can go into position 1, since all the other special features have been excluded from that place. But that brings the Cord in position 2 and the car with the chromed spare-tire cover in 3 with it. Since the Cord is in position 2, the Dusenberg is not and must, therefore, be in position 4. This forces the Avanti to be in position 1 (and to have the plated engine) and, with that, the hood-statue in position 2 (and, so, to be the Cord). This leaves the second string of 3, starting with the Bugatti, and it has to go from position 3 rightward: 3 - Bugatti - chromed spare-tire cover, 4 - monogrammed door - Dusenberg, 5 - eel-skin upholstery. By default, this last has to be the Edsel.

Using the previous information, we can determine that (A) must be wrong because the Avanti is on an end of the row but the monogrammed doors are on a car between two others—the Bugatti and the car with eel-skin upholstery. (B) has to be wrong because the Bugatti is just left of the car with monogrammed doors. (C) is wrong because, were it correct, the car to its right would have both the eel-skin upholstery and the chromed spare-tire cover, contrary to the condition that each car has just one feature. Finally, (E) must be wrong, for if the Edsel has the monogrammed door and so is just right of the Bugatti, the two ordering patterns would have to combine as eC(cB)(dE)u. (The other order would make the third car in order have both the plated engine and the eel-skin upholstery.) But then the Avanti must be in position 1 (or else the Edsel would have the hood statue as well as the monogrammed door). But that means that the Dusenberg has to be in position 4, which the Edsel already occupies. Since this is impossible, the Edsel cannot have the monogrammed door, so (E) is wrong. This leaves only (D) as correct.

4.   **(B)**   is the correct answer. To answer this question, first draw a diagram of the house two boxes wide and three boxes deep. Number the box on the front left 1, the one on the front right 2, the middle left 3, the middle right 4, the back left 5, and the back right 6. The yellow room is at the front on the left, so put a y at the bottom of box 1. The master bedroom is at the front on the right, so put MB at the top of box 2. The red room is directly behind the master bedroom, so put an r at the bottom of box 4. The kitchen is not yellow, so it is not at the front of the house. The kitchen is in front of the utility room, so it must be in the second row of rooms, while the utility room must be at the back of the house. Since the kitchen is to the left of the utility room, it must be box 3, so put K at the top of that box. The utility room is behind and to the right of the kitchen, so it must be box 6. Put UR at the top of box 6. The small bedroom is at the back of the house, so it is box 5. Put SB in box 5. The dining room is to the right of the brown room. Boxes 2 and 6 are already assigned, leaving 4 as the only unassigned room on the right. The dining room must be box 4, which is red.

(A) is incorrect because the dining room is on the right side, while the yellow room is on the left side of the house. (C) is incorrect because the conditions state that the dining room is to the right of the brown room. (D) is incorrect because there is insufficient information given to establish which room is beige.

5.   **(E)**   is the correct answer. In order to answer the question, draw a grid six boxes long by five boxes wide. Across the side put the letters A – F. Across the top put the abbreviations for each of the ethnic origins. Now we can begin to apply the conditions to the grid. Condition 3 states that D is Swedish. Place an O in the box for Swedish beside D, and place an X in each of the other boxes beside D, since each person has a single ethnic origin. Since the two people in each couple are not of the same ethnic origin, we can put an X in the Swedish box for E. Condition 4 says that neither A nor E is Scandinavian, so we can put an X in the Norwegian and Swedish boxes for A and E. Now we are ready to read the question. It asks which of the following MUST be true, so we can eliminate any answer which might or might not be true.

(A) is incorrect because we can see from our grid that A could be Native American, C could be Norwegian, and E could be African-American (remember, no two men can have the same ethnic origin). (B) is incorrect because F is Native American and we do not have sufficient information to determine the ethnic origin of B. (C) is incorrect because C might be Norwegian. (D) is incorrect because D is Norwegian and B might be Norwegian or Swedish. (E) is correct because person E is not Native American since F is, and person E is not Swedish or Norwegian since condition 4 prevents it. That means (E) must be African-American or Italian.

TYPE 2: Conditional Relationship Questions

Conditional relationship questions require you to identify how certain actions are related to or affect other actions, or how certain people's actions affect others' actions.

EXAMPLE

Curly is a ringmaster of a one-ring circus, and he must decide what acts will perform during this Saturday's matinee. The matinee runs for only one hour, and acts must be scheduled according to how long they take to set up, perform, and take down. He is considering six acts for the matinee: the knife-thrower, the trapeze artists, the clowns, Dynamo the Human Cannonball, the elephants, and finally, Pogo the Dancing Dog.

CONDITIONS/CLUES

1. Either Dynamo the Human Cannonball or the clowns must perform, as both acts draw big crowds and hence big profits.

2. If the knife-thrower performs, then there won't be time for the trapeze artists to perform.

3. If the elephants perform, then the trapeze artists will not be able to perform because of set-up problems.

4. Either the elephants or Pogo the Dancing Dog must perform, since there must be at least one animal act for the children in the audience.

5. If the trapeze artists do not perform, then the clowns will not be able to perform, since the clown act is tied into the trapeze act.

6. As it turns out, Dynamo the Human Cannonball will not perform, as he broke both arms in an automobile accident.

QUESTION

2. Which one of the following statements is true?

    (A) The clowns, the elephants, and the trapeze artists will perform in the Saturday matinee.

(B) Only the clowns and the trapeze artists will perform in the Saturday matinee.

(C) Only the elephants and the clowns will perform in Saturday's matinee.

(D) Only the clowns, the trapeze artists, and Pogo the Dancing Dog will perform in Saturday's matinee.

(E) Only Pogo the Dancing Dog and the knife-thrower will perform in Saturday's matinee.

After you have read through the passage and the conditions/clues and have determined that you are being presented with a conditional relationship question, that is, a question where you are asked to determine how certain actions will affect other actions, the next step is to determine if any of the conditions/clues or conclusions that follow from the conditions/clues have any terms in common. What are terms? They are words or groups of words that express a meaning. For example, in the above set of conditions, condition #1 has a term in common with condition #6, and that term is "Dynamo the Human Cannonball." Grouping these two conditions together we get:

1. Either Dynamo the Human Cannonball or the clowns must perform; and

6. As it turns out, Dynamo the Human Cannonball can't perform.

Now ask yourself what conclusion follows from these two conditions/clues. Note that in this type of question we do not go through each condition separately and determine what conclusions follow, as we do with some other types of questions; rather we ask what conclusions follow from pairs or groups of conditions. In this case the conclusion that follows is:

CONCLUSION #1

The clowns must perform.

How do we know this? Well, if either Dynamo or the clowns MUST perform, and since Dynamo will not perform, we know that the clowns must perform. Next we can pair conclusion #1 with condition #5, as they have the term "clowns" in common:

5. If the trapeze artists do not perform, then the clowns will not be able to perform, since the clown act is tied into the trapeze act.

Conclusion 1: The clowns must perform.

What follows from this pair?

CONCLUSION #2

It follows that the trapeze artists will perform.

Note that if one of these acts performs, the other must perform as well, since the acts are tied together. Now we can group conclusion #2 with conditions #2 and #3, which all have the term "trapeze artists" in common:

2. If the knife-thrower performs, then there won't be time for the trapeze artists to perform; and

3. If the elephants perform, then the trapeze artists will not be able to perform because of set-up problems.

Conclusion 2: The trapeze artists will perform.

Since we know that the trapeze artists WILL perform, and because of time limitations in condition #2 and set-up problems in condition #3, we can conclude:

CONCLUSION #3

The knife-thrower will not perform.

CONCLUSION #4

The elephants will not perform.

The only condition that has not been examined is condition #4. Note that both it and conclusion #4 have the term "elephants" in common.

4. Either the elephants or Pogo the Dancing Dog must perform.

Conclusion 4: The elephants will not perform.

From this pair we can conclude that:

CONCLUSION #5

Pogo the Dancing Dog must perform, since at least one animal act is needed to satisfy the children in the audience.

From the above, then, we know that the clowns, the trapeze artists, and Pogo the Dancing Dog will perform, and that the knife-thrower, the elephants, and Dynamo the Human Cannonball will not. The correct answer to the question is (D). Only the clowns, the trapeze artists, and Pogo the Dancing Dog will perform in Saturday's matinee.

In sum, use the following steps in approaching conditional relationship questions.

1. Carefully read through the passage and the conditions/clues.

2. Note what conditions/clues have terms in common, and group those that have terms in common together.

3. Ask yourself what conclusions follow from those pairs/groups.

4. Note if any conclusions you arrive at have any terms in common with any of the conditions/clues. If so, group those together as well and determine what further conclusions follow.

5. Be sure to work with what you are given. Do not impose your own assumptions or beliefs on any of the conditions/clues.

6. Note that in this type of problem, it is not necessary to draw a diagram or a chart.

➤ SHORTCUT

Once you have become proficient at using the methods of solving the conditional relationship type of analytical reasoning problems, you may find using symbolic notation is helpful as a way to speed up your work.

Symbolic notation is simply putting the words of the problem into shorthand which is easier and quicker to understand. Also, the actual process of "translating" problems into symbolic notation will help you comprehend more clearly the methods you are using to solve the problems.

This is an alternative means to solving the problem—if you find symbolic notation too difficult and confusing, it will probably hinder you more than help you, so don't even worry about it. It is not necessary to use symbolic notation to solve analytical reasoning problems; however, it may help you solve them faster, if you already have a good grasp on the methods described in the review section.

The symbols you will use are as follows:

$$\& \text{ (ampersand)} = \text{"AND"}$$

$$V = \text{"OR"}$$

$$\sim \text{ (tilde)} = \text{"NOT"}$$

$$\rightarrow = \text{"IMPLIES" OR "IF,THEN"}$$

You may also use the letters of the alphabet to stand for any item, situation, or relationship you wish. For instance:

LET

A = Alan brings the flowers to Margo's wedding.

B = Bernice brings the flowers.

A & B = Alan AND Bernice bring flowers.

A V B = Alan OR Bernice bring flowers.

A $\rightarrow$ $\sim$ B = IF Alan brings flowers, THEN Bernice will NOT bring flowers.

Let's take one of the sample problems from the review.

Betty, Eva, and Maria were planning on going to a party together. However, the day before the party, two of the women had an argument, such that the following conditions resulted:

1. If Betty went, then Maria did not go.

2. Eva went only if Betty went.

3. If Maria went, then either Betty or Eva did not go.

4. Maria went to the party.

First, we need to figure out our key.

LET

B = Betty went to the party.

E = Eva went to the party.

M = Maria went to the party.

Now, let's translate the conditions using our symbols.

1. B→ ~M

2. B→ E

3. M→ (~B V ~E)

4. M

Condition #4 gives us the information we need to uncover who actually went to the party. Since we know that M is true (Maria went to the party), we use this information to change condition #1,

B→ ~M

which also means

M→ ~B

since saying "If Betty went to the party, then Maria did not go" is the same as saying "If Maria went to the party, then Betty did not go." Therefore, since we know that M is true, we also know that B is NOT true, that Betty did NOT go to the party.

What about Eva? Well, condition #2,

B→ E

can also be said as

~B→ ~E

since Eva would not go without Betty. Since we know that ~B is true, we now know that ~E is also true, so Eva did not go either.

To solve the circus problem, you may use symbolic notation as well. Here are the conditions translated into symbols:

K = Knife-thrower performs.   T = Trapeze artists perform.

C = Clowns perform.   D = Dynamo performs.

E = Elephants perform.   P = Pogo performs.

1. D V C

2. K→ ~T

3. E→ ~T

4. E V P

5. ~T→ ~C

6. ~D

Again, we begin with the last statement and apply it to the others. Because condition #1 states

D V C,

and we know the ~D is true, then C must be true. Next, we have to skip to a condition that includes C or D, which brings us to condition #5, which we will restate to fit the conclusions we have already drawn:

C→ T

Therefore, T must be true. We return to condition #2, which can be stated as

T→ ~K.

This tells us that K is NOT true, since T is true. From condition #3, we learn that E is NOT true, using the same reasoning. Finally, since condition #4 states that either E or P must be true, and we already know that E is NOT true, P is true.

So C (the clowns), T (the trapeze artists), and P (Pogo) are all performing in the show.

Try using symbolic notation to help you solve your conditional relationship questions faster. If it does not help you, or if you have trouble understanding it, don't worry, it is not necessary to use symbolic notation to solve these problems, rather it is a shortcut for those who already understand the reasoning behind the solution methods.

Drill: Conditional Relationship

DIRECTIONS: Each group of questions in this section is based on a set of conditions. In answering some of the questions, it may be useful to draw a rough diagram. Choose the response that most accurately and completely answers each question.

1. Around Fashion Circle stand an A-frame house, a Bauhaus, a Cape Cod, a Dymaxion, an Ergonometric, a Federalist, a Georgian, and a Half-timbered, each on one of the ten evenly spaced lots of the outer periphery of the circle. Broad access roads fill the remaining two lots.

    The Federalist is directly across the circle from the Georgian, with an equal number of lots separating them on both sides of the circle.

    The A-frame and Half-timbered are next door to the Georgian.

    The A-frame and the Bauhaus are next door to each other.

    Neither access road is on a lot next door to the Federalist.

    If the Cap Cod is immediately to the left of the Federalist and the Dymaxion is two places to the right of the Georgian, which of the following must be true?

    (A) The Half-timbered house is next to an access road.

    (B) The Dymaxion is next door to the Federalist.

    (C) The Ergonometric is next door to the Cape Cod.

    (D) There is an access road immediately to the right of the Dymaxion.

    (E) The two access roads are next to each other.

2. Seated at the head of the Fraternal Frolic were, from left to right, Al, Bill, Charlie, Dave, and Ed. Each of them belonged to exactly two fraternal organizations—Lions, Elks, Masons, Kiwanis, and Odd Fellows. The following conditions held for the five men.

    The organizations fall into three groups: A, composed of Lions and Elks; B, composed of Kiwanis and Odd Fellows; and C, Masons alone.

    The two organizations each person belongs to come from two different groups.

    No person belonged to any organization to which a man sitting next to him belonged.

    Bill belonged to the Masons and the Odd Fellows.

    Ed belonged to the Lions.

    If only one of the men is both a Mason and in a Group B organization, which of the following must be true?

    (A)   No more than two of the men are Lions.

    (B)   No more than two of the men are Elks.

    (C)   No more than two of the men are in Kiwanis.

    (D)   No less than two of the men are both Masons and in Group A organizations.

    (E)   No less than two of the men are Odd Fellows.

3. Every Wednesday five salespeople—V, W, X, Y, and Z—check into the Dew Drop Inn.

    They always stay in rooms 201 through 206.

    Each takes a different room, but one of the rooms is not used by any of them.

    W always takes an odd-numbered room.

    Y always takes the third room in numerical order from those which the salespeople use.

    Z always has a higher numbered room than V, but none of the other salespeople takes a room between Z's and V's.

    If none of the salespeople takes room 201, which of the following must be true?

I.   If W takes room 203, Z takes room 206.

II. If Z takes room 203, W takes room 205.

III. X does not take room 205.

(A) I only

(B) II only

(C) III only

(D) I and II only

(E) I, II, and III

Questions 4 and 5 refer to the following passage.

The local high school offers five senior courses during first period: English, French, algebra, geometry, and home economics. Art, Barb, Cheryl, Dave, and Ed are making out their schedules and must choose which course to take first period.

If Art takes a math class, Cheryl must take a language class.

Ed has had all of the math courses and will not repeat them.

Barb will take English.

Dave and Ed will take the same course.

Art takes algebra.

Barb and Cheryl will not take the same course.

4.   Which of the following must be false?

(A)   Dave will not take geometry.

(B)   Cheryl will take French.

(C)   Ed will not take algebra.

(D)   Cheryl will take home economics.

(E)   Dave could take home economics.

5. If Dave and Ed take different courses and no two students will take the same course, which of the following must be true?

(A) Dave will take algebra, and Ed will take home economics.

(B) Dave will take home economics, and Ed will take French.

(C) Dave will take geometry, and Ed will take home economics.

(D) Dave will take home economics, and Ed will take geometry.

(E) Dave will take French, and Ed will take home economics.

Conditional Relationship
Detailed Explanations
of Answers

1. **(D)**   is the correct response. With these houses located, the map is

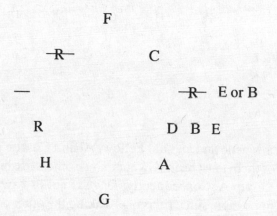

or maybe (since the sides for the A-frame and the Half-timbered were not given)

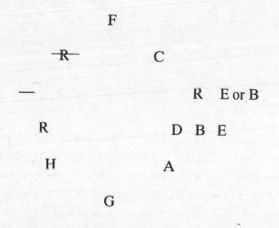

In either case, the Ergonometric and the Bauhaus must be in the two lots immediately right of the Federalist, since they have to go into adjoining lots with one of them in this place. The remaining two places must then be roads. Thus, (D), that a road runs immediately to the Dymaxion's right must be true and the correct answer. (A) is true in one arrangement of the Half-timbered and the A frame houses, but not the other and, so, does not have to be true. (B) must be false, since there are four places between the Georgian and the Federalist and the Dymaxion is only half-way along that space. (C) must be wrong because the given houses on the Cape Cod side of the Federalist leave only one lot, and the Ergonometric can go only where the Bauhaus can go next to it. Finally, (E) is false because the arrangement of houses does not allow a solid line of houses around either side to permit a double gap on the other.

2. **(B)** is the correct answer. The initial information, and some inferences from it, look like this

		A	B	C	D	E
A	L		n		n	y
	E		n			n
B	K	y	n	y	n	
	O	n	y	n		
C	M	n	y	n		

Since Bill is a Mason and an Odd Fellow, Al and Charlie can be either of these. Hence, both of them must be in Kiwanis, since otherwise both their memberships would be in Group A. Consequently, Dave is not in Kiwanis, since Charlie is. Dave is also not a Lion, since Ed is one. Taking the other conditions into account gives the following chart

		A	B	C	D	E
A	L		n	y	n	y
	E		n	n	y	n
B	K	y	n	y	n	
	O	n	y	n		
C	M	n	y	n		

Bill already is a Mason and in a Group B organization (namely, an Odd Fellow). The claim says, then, that Bill is the only one and so that Dave is not one also. Dave may, then, be either a Mason and an Elk or an Elk and an Odd Fellow, since he cannot be a Mason and an Odd Fellow. So, in any case, Dave is an Elk. But then, Charlie is not an Elk, because he is next to Dave. Bill and Ed are already given as not being Elks, so there can be at most one other Elk than Dave, Al. Thus, (B), that there are at most two Elks, is true. (A) is false, since Al could equally well be a Lion and, so, with the certified Lion, Ed, and Charlie, who must be a Lion because he cannot be an Elk, there might be three Lions. As for (C), Al and Charlie are already in Kiwanis and nothing prevents Ed from being one, too, though nothing forces it either. (D) must be wrong because only Dave or Ed could be a Mason and then only one of them, for they are next to each other. So, at most one man can be both a Mason and either a Lion (if Ed) or and an Elk (Dave). Finally (E) does not have to be true, for, while either Dave or Ed might be an Odd Fellow, both have other possibilities. For example, Dave might be a Mason and Ed in Kiwanis.

3.　**(E)**　is the correct response. The chart is as follows.

```
1      2      3      4      5      6
       W̶            W̶            W̶
                           V̶            VZ or VOZ
O             Y
```

Since the first place is empty, Y will be in room 204, the third in order of the used rooms. Thus, VZ can go into either 202-203 or into 205-206. In the first case, W will be 203 and Z will be 206, leaving X in room 202. Thus, I is true. In the second case, Z will be in 203 and W will be in 205, the remaining odd-numbered room, and X will be in 206. Thus, II is true also. In neither case will X be in 205—but in 206 in the first case and 202 in the second. Thus, claim III is also true. So, (E), that all three are true, is the correct answer. The others omit at least one true claim.

4.　**(D)**　is the correct answer. If Art takes a math class, Cheryl must take a language class. Since Art takes algebra, Cheryl must take a language. Barb and Cheryl will not take the same class, and Barb is taking English. That means that Cheryl must take French, not home economics. (A) is true, since Dave and Ed will take the same course, and Ed will not repeat any of the math courses. (B) is true for the reasons given above. (C) is true because Ed has had all of the math courses and will not repeat them. (E) is true because Dave will take the same course as Ed, and Ed will not take a math course. However, both could take any of the other courses, including home economics.

5.　**(C)**　is the correct response. As we established above, Art takes algebra, Barb takes English, and Cheryl takes French. Ed has completed his math courses and the only non-math course which is not taken is home economics. That leaves geometry for Dave to take. (A) is incorrect because Art is taking algebra, so Dave cannot take it. (B) is incorrect because Cheryl is taking French, so Ed cannot take it. (D) is incorrect because Ed has already completed all of the math courses. (E) is incorrect because Cheryl is taking French, so Dave cannot take it.

TYPE 3: Familial Relationship Questions

In familial relationship questions you will be given certain conditions concerning family members, and based on those conditions you will have to determine the relationships between those family members. The simplest way to approach such questions is to construct a chart or family tree that accurately reflects the relationships expressed in the conditions.

EXAMPLE

Mary and John Smith, following an old Sicilian tradition, named their six children in the following way.

CONDITIONS/CLUES

1. Their first child, a son, was named after the child's paternal grandfather. If their first child had been a daughter, she would have been named after her paternal grandmother.

2. Their second child, another son, was named after the child's maternal grandfather. If their second child had been a daughter, she would have been named after her maternal grandmother.

3. Their third child, a daughter, was named after one of the child's paternal aunts. If the child had been a son, he would have been named after one of his paternal uncles.

4. Their fourth child, a son, was named after one of the child's maternal uncles. Had this child been a daughter, she would have been named after one of her maternal aunts.

5. Their fifth child, another daughter, was named after one of the child's paternal aunts.

6. Their final child, a son, was named after one of the child's maternal uncles.

Mary and John Smith's children, from oldest to youngest, are Vincenzio, Vito, Michelle, Joseph, Catharine, and Anthony.

Note: Children of siblings may have the same first name.

The tradition results in many people in the extended family having the same first names.

Mary Smith has only two siblings.

John Smith has five siblings: two sisters and three brothers.

Their third child, Michelle, is married to a man who has two sisters.

QUESTION

3. If Mary and John Smith's daughter Michelle has four children, all daughters, what will her youngest daughter's name be if she follows this old Sicilian tradition?

   (A) Michelle   (D) Mary Jo

   (B) Mary   (E) Antonia

   (C) Catharine

As stated earlier, the easiest way to approach this type of problem is to construct a diagram or family tree which accurately depicts the relationships expressed in the conditions. Reading through the passage and conditions, we can conclude:

1. John's father was named Vincenzio, since John and Mary's first son was named Vincenzio. This is in accord with condition #1.

2. Mary's father was named Vito, since Mary and John's second child, a son, was named Vito. This is in accord with the second condition.

3. John's two sisters are named Catharine and Michelle, since John and Mary's third and fifth children, daughters, were named Michelle and Catharine, respectively. This is in accord with conditions #3 and #5.

Finally, we can conclude

4. Mary has two brothers, her only two siblings, and their names are Joseph and Anthony, respectively. This follows from conditions #4 and #6.

From these conclusions and what we have been given about John and Mary's children, we can construct the following diagram:

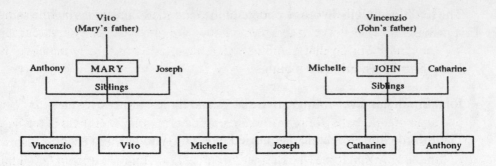

Looking at the diagram and the conditions, we can now answer the question. If Mary and John's daughter Michelle has four children, we can make the following conclusions:

1. It is not possible to determine the name of her first daughter, as the child must be named after the child's paternal grandmother (condition #1), and we have not been given this piece of information about Michelle's husband's family.

2. Michelle's second daughter, following condition #2, will be named Mary, after the child's maternal grandmother.

3. It is not possible to determine her third daughter's name, because again, we have not been given the names of Michelle's husband's sisters.

However, we can determine Michelle's fourth daughter's name. The fourth condition tells us that the fourth child is to be named after one of the child's maternal aunts, that is, after one of the child's mother's sisters. Since Michelle has only one sister, Catharine, her fourth daughter will be named Catharine. The correct answer to the question, then, is (C) Catharine.

In sum, use the following steps in answering familial relationship questions:

1. Carefully read through the passage and conditions, and determine if you have been given a familial relationship question.

2. Construct a diagram or family tree. Do this by first reading through a condition, and then doing that part of the diagram.

3. Keep in mind that you may not be able to construct a diagram by following the conditions in the order in which they are given. If necessary, regroup the conditions so that conditions that have terms or family members in common are grouped together.

4. Do not impose your own assumptions on this type of question. For example, perhaps your family does not name family members in the way described in this problem. Or perhaps you do not define "second cousins" in the way that it may be defined in a question you may encounter on the test. Do not argue with the conditions given to you. Rather take them as true and determine what conclusions follow from them.

Drill: Familial Relationship

DIRECTIONS: Each group of questions in this section is based on a set of conditions. In answering some of the questions, it may be useful to draw a rough diagram. Choose the response that most accurately and completely answers each question.

1. Pete is Ramon's father and Angela's son.

    Pete has more daughters than he has sons and he has more sons than he has sisters and all of his children come from his marriage to Sylvia.

    Rachel is Ramon's aunt and Pete's sister, and she has several children.

    Ramon's mother, Sylvia, has no siblings. Ramon has at least one brother.

    If Juan is Pete's brother, then Sylvia is Juan's

    (A) sister.   (D) niece.

    (B) sister-in-law.   (E) daughter.

    (C) aunt.

2. The noble tribe goes to the ball in a rainbow of body-concealing, hooded robes. Concealed within the red, orange, yellow, green, blue, indigo, and violet raiments were the Earl and his Countess, their son and their two daughters, the children's uncle, and the Earl's son-in-law. Because the family runs to a type, even in the choice of mates, it is not obvious who is who. However, it is known that:

    Orange and yellow conceal members of the same sex.

    Green and blue conceal members of different sexes.

    The person in indigo is older than the one in green.

    The person in yellow is not the father of the person in red.

    The red cape covers the married daughter.

If the people in yellow and blue are brothers, which of the following must be true?

(A)   The person in green is female.

(B)   The person in green is male.

(C)   The person in indigo is female.

(D)   The person in indigo is male.

(E)   The person in violet is female.

3.   King Kennels has developed a new kind of breeding program for producing show dogs. In this program the best configured male dog from a litter is bred to the best configured female from another litter. The exact relationship between the two dogs is this: the male's dam (mother) is the litter mate (sibling) of the female's sire (father). Caesar and Lady are bred and produce the kennel's first champion dog.

1.   Lady had one litter mate, Luke, a male.

2.   Patch, a female, was one of three litter mates sired by Dan.

3.   Mack was bred to Donette, a female, producing Luke and Lady.

4.   Gypsy, a female, produced a litter of three, including Patch, a female, and Brandy, a female.

5.   Cid, a male, was bred to Brandy, a female, producing Caesar and Tiny, a female.

6.   Mack is Brandy's litter mate.

7.   Patch was neutered before she had any pups.

8.   None of the dogs were bred to any but the dogs mentioned, and none produced more than one litter.

Which of the following is the sire of Mack?

(A)   Cid

(B)   Caesar

(C)   Luke

(D)   Dan

(E)   Impossible to tell because of insufficient information.

4. John, an avid reader all his life, wishes to leave his library to someone in his family who shares his love of books. Among his family members are:

    1. Ed, who is married to Fay;

    2. Doris, who is the daughter of Fred;

    3. Sue, who is married to Henry;

    4. Mary, who is the sister of John and the wife of Fred;

    5. Fay, who is the daughter-in-law of John;

    6. Nancy, who is Ed's mother; and

    7. Henry, who is the brother of Doris.

    John leaves the library to Doris, who is his

    (A) niece.   (D) daughter.

    (B) wife.   (E) wife's sister.

    (C) sister.

5. Sam Jones learns that he has a long lost brother living in another city. When Sam checks the telephone book for Joneses in that city, he finds 20 pages of them. Although he does not know his brother's first name or address, Sam has discovered a document which gives him vital information that will help him determine his brother's name. According to the document:

    1. Cindy is Sam's sister.

    2. Sharon is married to Pete and is the mother of Steve.

    3. Ben and Nate are brothers.

    4. Dot, who is married to Sam, is Ben's mother.

    5. Sam's mother is Rhonda.

    6. Dan and Ella are Cindy's paternal grandfather and grandmother.

    7. Dave's wife has two brothers.

    8. Steve is Cindy's nephew.

    9. Dave is Rhonda's son-in-law.

    10. Arnie is Dan's son.

None of the people have any brothers, sisters, or children who are not mentioned by name in the above conditions.

Based on the information in the document, we can determine that Sam's brother's name is

(A)   Dave.

(D)   Arnie.

(B)   Pete.

(E)   Ben.

(C)   Dan.

Familial Relationship
Detailed Explanations
of Answers

1.   **(B)**   is correct. These problems involve multiple relations, all centered on a family tree. Begin by diagramming all that you know about the family.

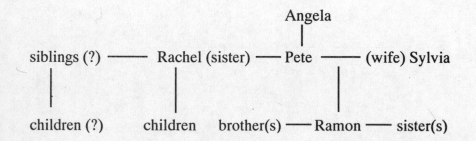

This question is simply one of family relations. The wife of one's brother is one's sister-in-law. Thus, (B) is the correct answer.

2.   **(A)**   is the correct response. The initial information is only

R   O   Y   G   B   I   V

m   e̶   M = e/s/u/i   F = c/m/d   I > G   O = Y   G ≠ B

F

(Capital letters for colors, lowercase for people: c = the Countess, d = the unmarried daughter, e = the Earl, i = the son-in-law, m = the married daughter, s = the son, u = the uncle.)

If the people in blue and yellow are brothers, then both are male. Since one of the people wearing blue or green is not male, that must be the person in green, who is, therefore, female, as (A) says. (B) has to be false, since (B) would have both the person in blue and the person in green, the same sex, against the original restriction. (C) might be true, as might both (D) and (E) together, because the wearers of indigo and violet have to be of different sexes. However, none of these latter three has to be true, as (A), the correct answer, does.

3.   **(D)**   is the correct answer. Using the clues given, construct a diagram. Condition 2 states that Patch was one of three litter mates. Condition 4 states that Patch and Brandy were litter mates. Dan is the sire, according to 2, and Gypsy is the dam, according to 4. In your diagram place Dan and Gypsy side by side, with Patch and Brandy below as offspring. Condition 6 states that Mack is Brandy's litter mate. So place Mack beside Patch and Brandy. Condition 3 states that Mack was bred to Donette, producing Luke and Lady. Place Donette beside Mack, with Luke and Lady below as offspring. Condition 5 states that Cid and Brandy produced Caesar and Tiny. Place Cid beside Brandy, with Caesar and Tiny below them. Your finished diagram should look like this:

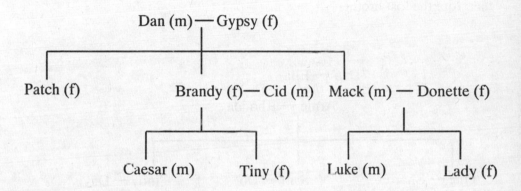

It is clear from the diagram that the sire of Mack is Dan.

4.   **(A)**   is the correct response. To answer the question construct a diagram. Start with Ed and Fay, who are married. Nancy is Ed's mother, while John is Fay's father-in-law. That means that John and Nancy are married and are Ed's parents. Mary is John's sister and Fred's wife. Doris is Fred's daughter, which makes her Nancy's daughter and, therefore, John's niece.

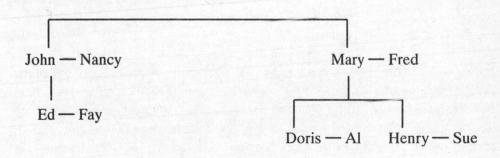

5.   **(B)**   is the correct answer. Begin your diagram with Cindy and Sam, who are siblings. According to condition 5, Sam's mother is Rhonda, so pencil her in above Sam and Cindy. Dot is Sam's wife and Ben's mother (condition 4), so Ben is Sam's son. Nate is Ben's brother (condition 3), so he is also the son of Sam and Dot. Dan and Ella are Cindy's paternal grandparents (condition 6), so they are the parents of Cindy and Sam's father. Arnie is Dan's son, so he is Cindy and Sam's father, and Rhonda's husband. Dave is Rhonda's son-in-law (condition 9), so he is Cindy's husband. Dave's wife, Cindy, has two brothers (condition 7). Steve is Cindy's nephew (condition 8). He is not Sam's son, since both of Sam's sons have been determined. Steve must be the son of the lost brother. Steve's mother is Sharon, who is married to Pete (condition 2). Pete is Steve's father and is therefore the lost brother.

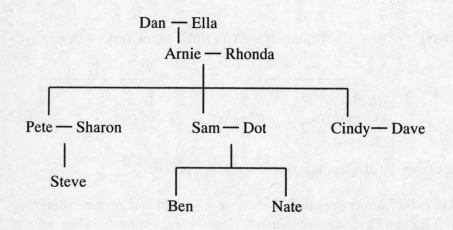

TYPE 4: Ordering Relationship Questions

Ordering relationship questions require that you determine the temporal order of events. Below is an example of such a question. Read through the passage, the conditions/clues, and the question. Then think about how you might go about solving this problem—that is, what method would you use? Next, think about why you chose that method. Try to solve this problem using your method, and then look at the solution below, which suggests two methods that can be used in approaching this type of problem.

EXAMPLE

It's Herbert's birthday, and six of his closest friends have been invited to his surprise birthday party: Adam, Ben, Carol, Dora, Edwin, and Fred.

Note: No one arrives at the same time, and "before" and "after" do not imply "immediately before" and "immediately after."

CONDITIONS/CLUES

1. Edwin arrives before Fred.

2. Dora arrives before Ben, but not before Carol.

3. Edwin arrives after Ben and after Carol.

4. Adam arrives before Ben.

QUESTION

Which of the following is one possible order of their arrival?

I.   Carol, Adam, Dora, Ben, Edwin, and Fred

II.   Carol, Dora, Adam, Ben, Edwin, and Fred

III. Adam, Carol, Dora, Ben, Edwin, and Fred

(A) I only

(D) II and III only

(B) II only

(E) I, II, and III

(C) I and II only

As you should do with all of the analytical reasoning questions on the test, first read through the passage and conditions and determine what type of relationship is being expressed. In this case you are asked to consider how Adam, Ben, Carol, Dora, Edwin, and Fred are related to each other regarding the order of their arrival at Herbert's birthday party. After you determine that the relationship being expressed is one of temporal ordering, then go on to the first question and determine if a chart or diagram is necessary to answer the question. In this case, a chart/diagram is not necessary. Note that the question asks you to determine possible orders of their arrival, and you are given three choices. The simplest way to approach this question, and the first method that we will use to solve this problem, is to read through each of the choices and see if it satisfies each of the conditions. If so, then it is a possible order of their arrival.

The three possible orders you are given are:

I. Carol, Adam, Dora, Ben, Edwin, and Fred

II. Carol, Dora, Adam, Ben, Edwin, and Fred

III. Adam, Carol, Dora, Ben, Edwin, and Fred

Which of these orders satisfies the required conditions?

The first condition states that Edwin arrives before Fred. As you can see, all three orders satisfy this condition.

The second condition states that Dora arrives before Ben, but not before Carol. Again, all three choices satisfy this condition.

The third condition states that Edwin arrives after Ben and after Carol. All three choices also satisfy this condition.

Finally, the fourth condition states that Adam arrives before Ben. This condition is also satisfied in each of the three orders given.

Since all four conditions are satisfied in each of the three choices, the correct answer is (E) I, II, and III.

This ordering relationship question was fairly simple. In this case, you did not have to go through each condition and determine what conclusions follow. However, you could have solved the problem by doing just that, and you may have to determine what conclusions follow on the actual test if you are given an ordering relationship question. Therefore, for practice and again to see this model of reasoning in action, we will solve this problem using a second method, and that is to read through each condition/clue carefully and determine what conclusions follow, and to keep track of those conclusions on a chart.

CONDITION/CLUE #1

Edwin arrives before Fred.

CONCLUSIONS

1. Fred does not arrive first.

2. Edwin does not arrive last.

These conclusions can be indicated on the chart, with "X" meaning "no" and "O" meaning "yes."

	First	Second	Third	Fourth	Fifth	Sixth
Adam						
Ben						
Carol						
Dora						
Edwin						X
Fred	X					

CONDITION/CLUE #2

Dora arrives before Ben, but not before Carol.

CONCLUSIONS

1. Ben does not arrive first.

2. Dora does not arrive first.

3. Dora does not arrive last.

4. Carol does not arrive last.

As indicated on the chart:

	First	Second	Third	Fourth	Fifth	Sixth
Adam						
Ben	X					
Carol						X
Dora	X					X
Edwin						X
Fred	X					

CONDITION/CLUE #3

Edwin arrives after Ben and after Carol.

CONCLUSIONS

1. Edwin does not arrive first.

2. Edwin does not arrive second, since he must arrive after Ben, and from condition #2, we know that Ben does not arrive first.

3. Ben does not arrive last.

4. Carol does not arrive last.

As indicated on the chart:

	First	Second	Third	Fourth	Fifth	Sixth
Adam						
Ben	X					X
Carol						X
Dora	X					X
Edwin	X	X				X
Fred	X					

CONDITION/CLUE #4

Adam arrives before Ben.

CONCLUSIONS

1. Ben does not arrive first (this is also derived from condition #2).

2. Adam does not arrive last.

	First	Second	Third	Fourth	Fifth	Sixth
Adam						X
Ben	X					X
Carol						X
Dora	X					X
Edwin	X	X				X
Fred	X					

Looking at the above chart, we can immediately see that:

1. Fred arrives last, and

2. Either Adam or Carol must arrive first.

Going back over the conditions and conclusions, and grouping those that concern Edwin together, we know that Edwin arrives before Fred, after Ben, and after Carol (conditions #1 and #3), and since both Dora and Adam arrive before Ben (conditions #2 and #4), we also know that Edwin arrives after Dora and after Adam.

Since Edwin arrives after Ben, after Dora, after Carol, and after Adam, we know that Edwin must be the fifth person to arrive at the party. This can be indicated on the chart:

	First	Second	Third	Fourth	Fifth	Sixth
Adam			X	X	X	X
Ben	X					X
Carol			X	X	X	X
Dora	X					X
Edwin	X	X	X	X	O	X
Fred	X	X	X	X	X	O

And since both Adam and Dora arrive before Ben, and since Dora arrives after Carol, we can also conclude that Carol arrives before Ben; that is, Ben arrives after Adam, Carol, and Dora. Thus, Ben must be the fourth person to arrive.

	First	Second	Third	Fourth	Fifth	Sixth
Adam			X	X	X	X
Ben	X	X	X	O	X	X
Carol			X	X	X	X
Dora	X			X	X	X
Edwin	X	X	X	X	O	X
Fred	X	X	X	X	X	O

Combining these conclusions with the fact that either Adam or Carol must arrive first, we arrive at the three possible orders given to us in the question. However, by following this model of reasoning, we also know why Ben, Edwin, and Fred must arrive fourth, fifth, and sixth respectively, and why Carol or Adam must arrive first.

Ordering relationship questions that appear on the test may require that you employ this more complex method. Note that this method requires deductive reasoning. But again, depending on the question, the first and simpler method presented may suffice.

In sum, use the following method in approaching ordering relationship questions:

1. Read the passage and conditions carefully and determine what relationship is expressed. Determine if you have been given an ordering relationship question.

2. Look at the questions and determine if it is necessary to go through each condition and determine what conclusions follow.

3. If possible, keep track of those conclusions via a chart or diagram.

4. Read through the choices that you are given in the questions, and determine which of the choices satisfies all of the given conditions.

5. Again, do not impose your own assumptions/beliefs on the conditions/clues, but rather take them as they are given to you.

Drill: Ordering Relationship

DIRECTIONS: Each group of questions in this section is based on a set of conditions. In answering some of the questions, it may be useful to draw a rough diagram. Choose the response that most accurately and completely answers each question.

1. The six sections of the village parade are filled by two bands, the volunteer fire department, the pony club, clowns, and dignitaries (the mayor, the constable, and the beauty queen) in open cars. The order of march must meet the following conditions:

    The clowns can be neither the first nor the last group.

    Neither band can be next to the pony club.

    The pony club must be just in front of the dignitaries.

    Which of the following arrangements is an acceptable order of the sections, from first to last place?

    (A) Band, ponies, dignitaries, fire department, clowns, band

    (B) Clowns, ponies, dignitaries, band, fire department, band

    (C) Band, clowns, ponies, dignitaries, band, fire department

    (D) Ponies, fire department, dignitaries, band, clowns, band

    (E) Band, fire department, clowns, dignitaries, ponies, band

2. The planning committee for a series of road rallies had seven checkpoints, T, U, V, W, X, Y, and Z, to use. Each rally would start from a checkpoint and each lap would end by checking in at a checkpoint. No lap passes any checkpoint other than the one which ends it. Each rally would end by checking in at the last checkpoint, not necessarily the same as the one from which the rally started. The checkpoints were connected directly — that is, without passing any other checkpoints between — by roads as follows:

U is connected directly to V and W.

V is connected directly to T and Y.

W is connected directly to V, X, Y, and Z.

Which of the following is a complete and accurate list of possible second checkpoints in a rally beginning from checkpoint Y?

(A) T, X, Z

(B) T, W, X, Z

(C) T, V, W, X, Z

(D) T, U, V, W, X, Z

(E) T, U, V, W, X, Y, Z

3. B, D, E, F, M, and P all ran in a foot race. At the halfway point in the race, the runner who came in first was in fifth place and the runner who was third at the halfway point came in fifth at the end. The runner in last place at the halfway point remained last at the end and the runner who led at the halfway mark came in second. In the final results, M finished two places ahead of E. E finished two places ahead of the runner who was in third at the halfway point. B finished behind M and ahead of E. The runner who was in third at the halfway mark finished three places behind B. F finished two places ahead of D.

Who came in first in the race?

(A) D

(B) E

(C) F

(D) M

(E) P

4. There are six players on the college tennis team: Adam, Jon, Ben, Randy, Duane, and Jeff. The coach ranks them in order from first to sixth at the beginning of the season. First is the best player, second the next best, and so forth.

1. Ben is behind Randy and Duane.

2. Adam is last.

3. Duane is ahead of Jeff.

4. Jon is ahead of Ben.

5. Jon is ahead of Randy.

What is the lowest position Duane can occupy?

(A) First   (D) Fourth

(B) Second   (E) Fifth

(C) Third

5.   Six boats have been entered in the annual Fourth of July Boat Auction. The auctioneer must decide in which order the boats — A, B, C, D, E, and F — will be auctioned off. In deciding the order, the auctioneer must observe the following restrictions:

1.   E cannot go third.

2.   Neither A nor D can go sixth or third.

3.   Either A or B must go immediately after D.

4.   F must go immediately after B.

5.   C must go before A.

6.   D must go before E.

If B goes first, which one of the following must be true?

(A) A goes sixth.   (D) A goes immediately before C.

(B) E goes fourth.   (E) E goes sixth.

(C) C goes last.

Ordering Relationship
Detailed Explanations
of Answers

1. **(C)** The basic information about the order of march is

1	2	3	4	5	6		
						b	= a band
						c	= clowns
~~c~~				~~c~~	bp	d	= dignitaries
						p	= ponies
						f	= fire department
~~d~~				p	pd	/	= not permitted in this space

The dignitaries cannot be in first place nor the ponies in last, since each requires the other next to it. The dignitaries after the ponies automatically keep the bands away.

List (C) clearly works: the clowns are in second place rather than at either end, and there they separate the band from the ponies that immediately precede the dignitaries. So, all the conditions on the order of march are met. In (A), however, a band is immediately in front of the ponies and in (B) the clowns come first, both forbidden placements. So, these two are not acceptable. Neither is (D), in which the fire department comes between the ponies and the dignitaries, nor (E), in which the ponies come after, rather than before, the dignitaries.

2. **(E)** The map must look something like this

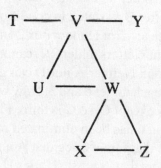

Since the rally rules do not forbid coming back to the starting point, Y is a possible second checkpoint, after a first stop at V or W. Thus, only (E) can be complete. It is also accurate: the following courses will reach each indicated checkpoint at the end of the second lap: VT, VU (or WU), WV, WX, WY (or VY), WZ. All of the other answers are accurate but incomplete, since they omit all the checkpoints they do not contain; additionally all checkpoints are reachable from Y in two steps.

3.　**(D)**　A chart should be developed indicating the position of each runner at the halfway point in the race and their final standings. After constructing such a chart, the letter of the runners can be constructed as follows:

Halfway B F P E M D

Finish　　M B E F P D

Since E finished two places ahead of the runner who ended in fifth place, E finished third. Since M finished two places ahead of E, M finished first. B finished behind M and ahead of E, therefore E was in second place. Since F finished two places ahead of D, D must be in last place and this leaves P to finish fifth.

4.　**(C)**　is the correct answer. The question asks about Duane's position, so we can look at the conditions to see which players must be behind Duane. Ben is behind Duane, as stated in condition 1. Adam is last, so he is behind Duane. Duane is ahead of Jeff. We cannot tell whether Jon and Randy are ahead of or behind Duane. If they are ahead of him, he would be third, the lowest position he can occupy.

5.　**(E)**　is the correct answer. Using the clues provided, construct a diagram. Across the top write 1-6 and down the side write A-F. Place an o below 1 for B, since we know B goes first. Place x's below 1 for the other letters, and place x's for positions 2-6 beside B. F must go immediately after B as stated in condition 4, so F is second. Fill in the diagram accordingly, with an o for F under box 2 and x's for the other positions beside F. Put x's for the other letters under 2. E cannot go third, as stated in condition 3, so x that position out. Neither A nor D can go sixth or third, as stated in condition 2. Place an x for each under 6 and 3. Now we see that position 3 has been eliminated for all letters except C, so C is third. Fill in the diagram accordingly. Now we see that position 6 has been eliminated for all letters except E, so E is sixth. After filling in the diagram we see that A and D are left, as are positions 4 and 5. Condition 3 tells us that A must go after D if B does not, so D is fourth and A is fifth. Checking our diagram against the answer choices, we see that only answer (E) is true.

TYPE 5: Spatial Relationship Questions

In spatial relationship questions, you will have to determine how objects are related in space.

EXAMPLE

Irving Park, a midsized city, has recently celebrated the opening of its new subway system. The system has the four following lines or routes.

CONDITIONS/CLUES

1. The Addams Line, which begins at point A, proceeds directly east passing through stops B and C, and ending at stop D.

2. The Green Line, which begins at point G, stops at points E and C, and ends at stop H.

3. The Red Line, which begins at point R, proceeds east and then due north where it stops at points B and E, respectively, and ends at stop F.

4. The Irving Line, which begins at point I, proceeds due north with a stop at C, and ends at stop J.

QUESTIONS

5a. Stop D is in what directional location to stop E?

   (A) Northeast   (D) Southeast

   (B) Southwest   (E) Directly north

   (C) West

5b. What stop is closest to stop H?

   (A) D   (D) R

   (B) J   (E) You can't tell based on the
                              information given.

   (C) A

After you have read through the passage and conditions/clues and have determined that you are dealing with a spatial relationship question, the next step you should take is to visualize, on paper, the relationships expressed in the conditions/clues. That is, draw a diagram that expresses the spatial relationship expressed in the conditions/clues.

The first condition concerns the Addams Line. We know that it begins at point A, proceeds directly east passing through stops B and C, and ends at stop D. Visually, this can be depicted as follows:

A————————B————————C————————————D

The second condition tells us that the Green Line begins at point G, stops at points E and C, and ends at point H. We need to skip this condition for now and come back to it, because we don't know where stop E is located. Note: With this type of question, it may not be possible to go through the conditions in the order in which they are given.

Going to the third condition, we know that the Red Line begins at point R, goes east and then north where it stops at points B and E, respectively, and then ends at point F.

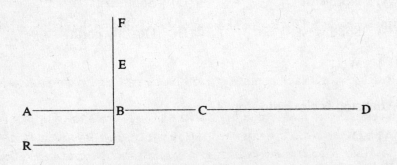

Now that we know that stop E is due north of B, we can go back to the second condition. Adding the Green Line to our diagram:

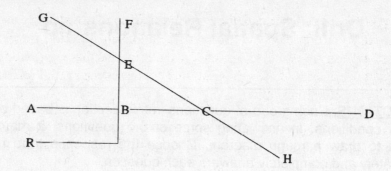

Finally, we go to the fourth condition, which tells us that the Irving Line begins at point I, proceeds due north with a stop at C, and ends at stop J. This results in the finished diagram.

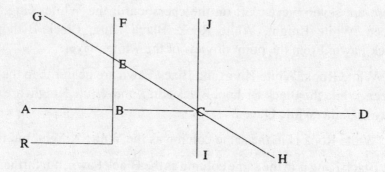

Looking at the diagram, we can easily see that stop D is southeast of stop E. The correct answer, then, is (D) Southeast. Also note that since we were given no measurements regarding distances in this problem, it is not possible to determine which stop is closest to stop H. The correct answer to the second question is (E). You can't tell based on the information given.

In sum, use the following method in approaching spatial relationship questions:

1. Read through each condition and do one part of the diagram at a time.

2. Keep in mind that it might not be possible to draw the diagram by going through the conditions in the order in which they are given. It may not be possible, for example, to diagram the relationship expressed in the second condition until you have diagrammed the relationships expressed in a later condition.

3. Again, do not impose your own assumptions or beliefs on the conditions/clues.

Drill: Spatial Relationship

> **DIRECTIONS**: Each group of questions in this section is based on a set of conditions. In answering some of the questions, it may be useful to draw a rough diagram. Choose the response that most accurately and completely answers each question.

1. There are seven pieces left on the chessboard: the White King, White Queen, White Knight, White Rook, Black King, Black Bishop, and Black Pawn. From the point of view of the white player,

    The White Rook, White King, and Black Pawn are nearer than the White Queen, while the Black Bishop, Black King, and White Knight are farther away than the White Queen.

    The White Rook is in the same column as the White Knight, but nearer.

    The Black King is in the same column as the Black Pawn, but farther away.

    Twice as many pieces are to the right of the White Queen as are to the left of the White Queen.

    The diagonal from the Black Pawn, going left and away from the white player, passes through the White Rook, White Queen, and Black Bishop, in order from near to far.

    The White King lies in what direction from the White Queen?

    (A) Toward the black player in the same column.

    (B) Away from the white player in the same column.

    (C) Toward the white player in the same column.

    (D) Toward the white player and to the right

    (E) Away from the white player and to the right.

2. Corporation M has established a chain of its Gas-M-Fast minimarts in state A. There are seven of the stores—C, D, E, F, G, H, and I—which are connected by three major routes—One, Two, and Three.

   1. Route Three runs from northeast to southwest, passing first by store H, then by I, then by D, and finally by store F.

   2. Route One runs from east to west, passing by store I, then by store C, then by store E.

   3. Route Two runs from north to south, passing first by store G, then by C, and finally by store D.

   Store H is in what directional location to store C?

   (A) Directly north

   (B) Directly south

   (C) Northeast

   (D) Northwest

   (E) Southeast

3. TIP Suppliers provide raw materials to five factories in its area. TIP ships the raw materials three times weekly—Monday, Wednesday, and Thursday—from its warehouse in the area. The locations of the factories and the warehouse are described by the following:

   1. The black factory is 10 miles west of the warehouse.

   2. The orange factory is two miles north of the blue factory.

   3. The purple factory is three miles north of the black factory.

   4. The white factory is two miles east and three miles north of the warehouse.

   5. The blue factory is 13 miles south of the purple factory.

   If the warehouse cannot ship to the south on Wednesday or the west on Thursday, what is the maximum number of factories that could receive shipments on those days?

   (A) Three on Wednesday, one on Thursday

   (B) Three on Wednesday, three on Thursday

   (C) Four on Wednesday, two on Thursday

   (D) Two on Wednesday, three on Thursday

   (E) Three on Wednesday, two on Thursday

Questions 4 and 5 are based on the following.

There are exactly seven people—Jim, Bill, Adam Chet, Dave, Mike, and Paul—sitting in a row in a theater, from left to right.

1. Paul is not first or last.

2. Jim is sitting fourth from the left.

3. Adam is sitting next to Jim.

4. Mike is sitting to the right of both Jim and Adam but to the left of Bill.

4. Which of the following could be sitting in the chair farthest to the right?

(A) Jim   (D) Mike

(B) Adam   (E) Paul

(C) Chet

5. If Chet sits immediately to the left of Jim, which one of the following statements must be false?

(A) Dave sits next to Chet.   (D) Mike sits next to Adam.

(B) Dave sits next to Paul.   (E) Paul sits next to Chet.

(C) Mike sits next to Bill.

Spatial Relationship
Detailed Explanations
of Answers

1.   **(C)**   Original set up of the schematic

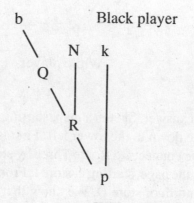

Only items connected by lines are placed correctly relative to one another, except that position relative to the White Queen—left or right, nearer to or farther from the white player is also set.

The White King is given as nearer to the white player than the White Queen, so the cases which place it farther away, (B) and (E), must be wrong. The diagram above shows that four pieces are to the right of the White Queen and it is given that twice as many pieces are to the right as to the left of the White Queen. So, there must be at least two pieces to the left of the White Queen. Only the Black Bishop is shown on the left and only the White King remains to be placed, so it must be on the left as well. So, the White King lies toward the white player from the White Queen and to the left, (C). The fact that there are only six pieces besides the White Queen on the board and that they are divided into those left and those right of the White Queen, with all accounted for, means that none are in the same column as the White Queen. Thus, neither (A) nor (B) can be correct. The fact that the White King must be to the left of the White Queen, as argued above, means that (D) and (E), which have it to the right of the White Queen, are not correct.

The final chart must be:

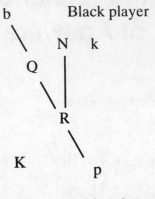

Black player

White player

2. **(C)** is the correct answer. Sketch a map, starting with Route Three. From the top right draw a line down to the lower left. First is store H, then I, then D, and finally F. Route One connects to Route Three by store I, so draw Route One from right to left across the page, starting at store I. From condition 3, we can see that store C is directly north of store D. We know that store E is west of C, but we cannot tell how far. Route Two runs from north to south, going first by G, then by C, then by D. Clearly, Routes One and Two intersect by store C, while Routes One and Three intersect by stores D and I. The finished map will look like this:

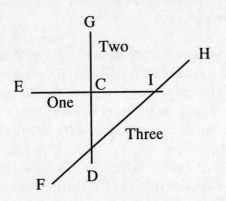

The map clearly shows store H is northeast of store C.

3.　**(A)**　is the correct answer. To correctly answer the question draw a map of the factories and warehouse. Start with the black factory west of the warehouse. Condition 2 does not help us yet. Condition 3 places the purple factory north of the black factory. Condition 4 places the white factory north and east of the warehouse. The blue factory is 13 miles south of the purple factory, which places it 10 miles south of the black factory and ten miles west of the warehouse. Condition 2 places the orange factory two miles north of the blue factory, thus also eight miles south of the black factory. The complete map looks like this:

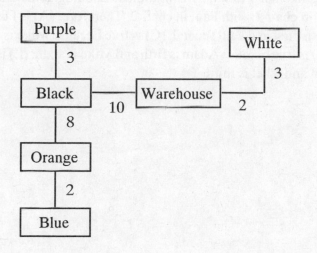

Now by looking at the map we can answer the question. We see that two factories are south of the warehouse, while three are even with or north of the warehouse. So three factories can receive shipments on Wednesday. Four factories are west of the warehouse, and only one even with or to the east, the white factory. Therefore, only one factory can receive a shipment on Thursday.

4.　**(C)**　is the correct answer. Construct a diagram with 1-7 across the top and the names of the people down the left. Jim is seated in the fourth chair (condition 2), so place an O there and X's in the other boxes for Jim. Also, place X's in box four for the other persons. Adam is sitting next to Jim (condition 3), so place question marks in boxes 3 and 5 for Adam. Place X's in boxes 1, 2, 6, and 7 for Adam, since those are not next to Jim. Paul is not first or last (condition 1), so place X's in those boxes for Paul. Mike is sitting to the right of Jim and Adam (condition 4), which could be chairs 5, 6, or 7. But he is to the left of Bill, which means he cannot sit in the last chair. Place question marks in 5 and 6 for Mike and an X in 7. Bill is sitting to the right of Mike (condition 4), which must be chair 6 or 7. Place question marks in those boxes and X's in the other boxes for Bill.

Now, by looking at the diagram we can see that only Chet, Dave, or Bill can be sitting in chair 7. Dave and Bill are not answer choices, so the answer must be Chet.

5.   **(A)**   is the correct answer. Remember that the question asks which answer choice must be false. Looking back at our diagram for this passage, we will now place an O in box 3 for Chet, and X's in the other boxes for Chet. We can also place X's in box 3 for the other people. Adam must be sitting to the right of Jim to satisfy condition 3. Mike must be sitting in chair 6 to satisfy condition 4. Bill must be sitting in chair 7 to satisfy condition 4. Looking at the diagram, we see that Dave sits in chair 1, with Paul in chair 2. Therefore, (A) is false. (B) is true because Dave is first and Paul second. (C) is true because Mike is sixth and Bill is seventh. (D) is true because Adam is fifth and Mike is sixth. (E) is true because Paul is second and Chet is third.

TYPE 6: Time Assignment Relationship Questions

Time assignment questions require you to identify relationships regarding dates and time blocks. That is, given certain dates and/or time blocks, events/people, and conditions linking the two, you must determine who or what goes in each time block.

EXAMPLE

A television executive in charge of programming is considering two possible lineups of five new shows for the new season. When the lineups are completed, he will present both to the Vice-President of Programming for approval. However, at present only one lineup is completed; the other is only partially completed. The five new shows that will go into the lineups are the following: a news show, a situation comedy, a detective drama, a musical/variety show, and a nighttime soap.

Each show is an hour long, and the time slots are 6:00, 7:00, 8:00, 9:00, and 10:00.

CONDITIONS/CLUES

1. In both of the lineups, the drama will be shown in the 7:00 time slot.

2. The news show will be on at 10:00 in only one of the lineups.

3. In both of the lineups, the nighttime soap will immediately follow the musical/variety show.

Again, one lineup is complete; the other lineup is only partially complete.

QUESTIONS

6a. Which of the following statements about the completed lineup is false?

(A) The situation comedy will be in the 6:00 time block.

(B) The musical/variety show will be in the 8:00 time block.

(C) The nighttime soap will be in the 9:00 time block.

(D) The situation comedy will be in the 8:00 time block.

(E) The news show will be in the 10:00 time block.

6b.   Which of the following statements about the incomplete lineup is false?

(A)   Either the news show or the situation comedy can appear in the 6:00 time block.

(B)   Either the musical/variety show, the news show, or the situation comedy can appear in the 8:00 time block.

(C)   Neither the situation comedy nor the news show can appear in the 9:00 time block.

(D)   Either the situation comedy or the news show can appear in the 9:00 time block.

(E)   The nighttime soap cannot appear in the 8:00 time block.

After reading through the passage and determining that you are being presented with a time assignment relationship question, the next step is to go through each condition and construct a chart—in this case two charts, one for the completed lineup and one for the incomplete lineup—to reflect the relationship expressed in each condition:

	6:00	7:00	8:00	9:00	10:00
Lineup #1					
Lineup #2					

CONDITION/CLUE #1

In both lineups, the drama show will be shown in the 7:00 time slot.

	6:00	7:00	8:00	9:00	10:00
Lineup #1		drama			
Lineup #2		drama			

CONDITION/CLUE #2

The news show will be on at 10:00 in only one of the lineups.

	6:00	7:00	8:00	9:00	10:00
Lineup #1		drama			news
Lineup #2		drama			

CONDITION/CLUE #3

In both lineups, the nighttime soap will immediately follow the musical/variety show.

From this condition and from looking at the above chart, we can deduce that since the drama show immediately follows the 6:00 time slot, then

1. Neither the musical/variety show nor the nighttime soap can appear in the 6:00 time block in either lineup, and so in the first lineup.

2. The musical/variety show must appear in the 8:00 time block and the nighttime soap must appear in the 9:00 time block.

	6:00	7:00	8:00	9:00	10:00
Lineup #1	not m.v. not soap	drama	mus. var.	soap	news
Lineup #2	not m.v. not soap	drama			

We can also deduce that:

3. The situation comedy must appear in the 6:00 time block in the first lineup.

Lineup #1	6:00	7:00	8:00	9:00	10:00
	Sit. Com.	drama	mus. var.	soap	news

As you can see from the above chart, the first lineup is the completed lineup. The correct answer to the first question, then, is (D). The situation comedy will be in the 8:00 time block.

However, determining the second lineup (the incomplete lineup) is not as easy. We know from the above that:

1. Neither the musical/variety show nor the nighttime soap can appear in the 6:00 time block.

Lineup #2	6:00	7:00	8:00	9:00	10:00
	not m.v. not soap	drama			

We also know from condition #3 that the nighttime soap immediately follows the musical/variety show. From this we can conclude:

4. The nighttime soap cannot follow the drama, and therefore cannot appear in the 8:00 time block.

Lineup #2	6:00	7:00	8:00	9:00	10:00
	not m.v. not soap	drama	not soap		

We can also conclude that:

5. The musical/variety show cannot appear in the 10:00 time block, since the soap must follow it, and the 10:00 time block is the last block.

Lineup #2	6:00	7:00	8:00	9:00	10:00
	not m.v. not soap	drama	not soap		not m.v.

By the process of elimination, or deduction, we can draw the following conclusions:

6. Either the news show or the situation comedy can appear in the 6:00 time block.

7. Either the musical/variety show, the news show, or the situation comedy can appear in the 8:00 time block.

8. Neither the situation comedy nor the news show can appear in the 9:00 time block, since if they did it would not be possible for the nighttime soap to immediately follow the musical/variety show (condition #3).

From conclusion #8 and the fact that the drama is in the 7:00 time block, it follows that:

9. Either the musical/variety show or the nighttime soap is in the 9:00 time block.

Lineup #2	6:00	7:00	8:00	9:00	10:00
	news or sit. com.	drama	m.v. or news or sit. com.	m.v. or soap	

and finally,

    10. Either the situation comedy or the soap can appear in the 10:00 time block, but not the news show (condition #2).

From the above, you can see that the correct answer to the second question concerning the incomplete lineup is (D). Either the situation comedy or the news show can appear in the 9:00 time block. That is, it is false that either the situation comedy or the news show can appear in the 9:00 time block.

In sum, use the following method in answering time assignment relationship questions:

1. Carefully read through the passage and the conditions/clues.

2. Construct a chart, and go through each condition/clue, accurately filling in the chart.

3. As you go through each condition and fill in the chart, ask yourself what conclusions follow from each condition/clue, and make note of these on the chart as well.

4. Again, do not impose your own assumptions/beliefs on the conditions or the questions, but take what is given to you as true.

Drill: Time Assignment Relationship

DIRECTIONS: Each group of questions in this section is based on a set of conditions. In answering some of the questions, it may be useful to draw a rough diagram. Choose the response that most accurately and completely answers each question.

1. Five children, A, B, C, D, and E, attend nursery school. There are five different play activities, 1, 2, 3, 4, and 5. All children will engage in four or more activities each day and must spend at least 20 minutes on any one activity once they begin it. No more than three children can be at any one activity at the same time. A and B cannot play together. C and D must always play together. The children are at school from 9 a.m. to 12 noon and take a 30 minute rest from 10:15 to 10:45 daily.

    Which of the following schedules would allow an appropriate assignment for D to be made?

    (A)   Activity 1 (9-9:30) A, C, D, E

    (B)   Activity 1 (9-9:30) A, C, E

    (C)   Activity 1 (10-10:30) A, C, D

    (D)   Activity 1 (9-9:30) B, E

    (E)   Activity 1 (9-9:30) A, B, C

Questions 2 and 3 refer to the following passage.

Darren, the foreman for company R, is in charge of the work schedules of seven employees—A, B, C, D, E, F, and G. Each employee must work four 10-hour days per week (Monday-Friday). In making out the schedule, Darren must observe the following conditions:

1.   A and D must work the same days, since they carpool.

2.   G cannot work Fridays.

3.   A cannot work Wednesdays.

4. D and F, who do not like each other, should work as few days together as possible.

5. E must work on Mondays.

6. At least four employees must work each day.

2. Darren could make all of the following schedules except:

(A) Only A, D, E, and G work on Monday.

(B) Only A, C, D, and G work on Tuesday.

(C) Only B, C, E, and G work on Wednesday.

(D) Only A, D, F, and G work on Thursday.

(E) Only F, D, E, and A work on Friday.

3. If E and F have the same schedule as G, and B and C take their day off one day after A, which of the following must be true?

(A) All employees work only on Monday.

(B) Six employees work on Thursday.

(C) Five employees work on Friday.

(D) All employees work on Tuesday.

(E) Six employees work on Wednesday.

4. Joan is the director of a summer youth program at the city park. She must schedule six events for each day for hourly time slots starting at 9:00 a.m. and ending at 4:00 p.m. Lunch is always from 12:00-1:00 p.m. and is not considered an event. Joan may choose from the following eight events: swimming, hiking, finger painting, napping, crafts, reading, softball, and badminton.

1. Badminton cannot be scheduled for Monday or Wednesday.

2. Napping must be scheduled each day at either 1:00 or 2:00 p.m.

3. Both hiking and swimming cannot be scheduled for the same day, but one of the two must be scheduled each day.

4. If softball is scheduled, reading must follow it immediately.

5. Badminton and softball cannot be scheduled for the same day, but one of the two must be scheduled each day.

6. Hiking and swimming, when scheduled, must be at 11:00 a.m., while softball and badminton, when scheduled, must be at 2:00 p.m.

7. Finger painting must precede crafts when the two are scheduled for the same day.

Which of the following must be true of the schedule for Monday?

(A) Finger painting will be scheduled at 2:00 p.m. and crafts at 3:00 p.m.

(B) Napping must be scheduled at 2:00 p.m.

(C) Swimming will be scheduled.

(D) Napping will be scheduled at 1:00 p.m. and reading at 3:00 p.m.

(E) Crafts will be at 10:00 a.m. and hiking at 11:00 a.m.

5. Mr. Sanders is interviewing candidates for a job in his department. There are nine candidates, five women and four men. The women are Abby, Betty, Clara, Demi, and Edie. The men are Zeke, Yosef, Wade, and Vic. Mr. Sanders has from Monday through Friday to complete his interviews.

1. No more than three people can be interviewed in a day.

2. Only women can be interviewed on Monday and Thursday. Only men can be interviewed on Tuesday and Wednesday.

3. Zeke must be interviewed before Edie and Betty.

4. No one is interviewed more than once.

5. Abby, Clara, and Demi must be interviewed on Monday.

6. Betty cannot be interviewed on Thursday.

7. At least one person must be interviewed each day.

8. Vic must be interviewed last.

9. Yosef and Wade must be interviewed on the same day.

Which of the following must be true?

(A)   Edie, Betty, and Vic are interviewed on Friday.

(B)   Only Zeke is interviewed on Wednesday.

(C)   Wade and Zeke are interviewed on different days.

(D)   Wade and Yosef are interviewed on Wednesday.

(E)   Wade and Yosef are interviewed on Tuesday.

Time Assignment Relationship
Detailed Explanations
of Answers

1. **(D)** is the correct answer. The answer to this question requires careful reading of the constraints described in the passage. After understanding these constraints, then the incorrect choices can be eliminated from the question. Since the factor that eliminates incorrect responses is usually easier to detect, it will usually be more expedient to eliminate the incorrect answers than to find the correct answer first. Choice (A) is deleted because four pupils are assigned to this time; choice (B) separates C and D who must be together; choice (C) includes the rest time; and choice (E) also separates C and D. Choice (D) is acceptable for it would leave pupils A, C, and D to engage in another activity together at this time.

2. **(C)** is the correct answer. Remember that the question asks which of the schedules do not meet the conditions. To answer the question, construct a diagram, with the days of the week across the top and A-G down the side. Condition 1 does not help us immediately, so go to 2. G cannot work Fridays, so put an X in that box. Since each employee must work at least four days, G must work every other day except Friday. Put an O under the other days of the week for G. A cannot work Wednesdays, so put an X in Wednesday for A. A must work the other four days, so put O's under the other days for A. Now we can go back to condition 1. A has the same schedule as D, so put an X under Wednesday for D, and O's under the other days for D. D and F work together as little as possible, which means that the one day when D is gone F will work. So put an O under Wednesday for F. E must work on Mondays, so put an O under Monday for E. The finished diagram looks like this:

	M	T	W	Th	F
A	O	O	X	O	O
B					
C					
D	O	O	X	O	O
E	O				
F			O		
G	O	O	O	O	X

Now we are ready to check the answer choices against the diagram. We see that only choice (C) would violate the conditions, since F must work on Wednesday.

3.   **(D)**   is the correct answer. Going back to our diagram, we can now fill in the new information. E and F have the same schedule as G, which means they work Monday-Thursday and are off Friday. B and C are off the day after A, which means they are off Thursday and work the other days. This new information fills in the diagram completely. It looks like this:

	M	T	W	Th	F
A	O	O	X	O	O
B	O	O	O	X	O
C	O	O	O	X	O
D	O	O	X	O	O
E	O	O	O	O	X
F	O	O	O	O	X
G	O	O	O	O	X

Looking at the diagram, we see that (A) is incorrect because all employees work Monday and Tuesday. (B) is incorrect because seven employees do not work Thursday, (B and C have the day off) which means that only five employees work that day. (C) is incorrect because E, F, and G do not work Friday, so only four work that day. All employees work on Tuesday, which makes (D) the correct answer. D and A do not work Wednesday, so only five employees work that day.

4.   **(D)**   is the correct answer. To answer the question draw a diagram with the events across the top and the time slots from 9:00 to 3:00 down the left side. Place X's in the 12:00 time slot for all events, since that slot is reserved for lunch. Badminton cannot be scheduled for Monday (condition 1) so places X's in all time slots under badminton. Since badminton cannot be scheduled, softball must be scheduled (condition 5), and it must be scheduled at 2:00 (condition 6). Place an O in the 2:00 time slot for softball. Place X's in all other time slots for softball, and place X's in all 2:00 time slots for the other events. Reading must immediately follow softball (condition 4), so place an O in the 3:00 time slot for reading, and place X's in other time slots for reading and in all other 3:00 time slots. Either swimming or hiking must be scheduled (condition 3), and whichever one it is has to be at 11:00. Since we cannot tell from the conditions which will be scheduled, place question marks for swimming and hiking in the 11:00 time slot. Place X's in all other time slots for swimming and hiking, and place X's for all other events in the 11:00 time slot. Napping must be at either 1:00 or 2:00 (condition 2). Since the 2:00 time slot is taken by softball, napping must be at 1:00. Place an O in the 1:00 time slot for napping. Place an X in all other time slots for napping, and place X's in the 1:00 time slot for all other events. Now the only empty time slots are at 9:00 and 10:00 for finger painting and crafts. Since finger painting must precede crafts, finger painting must be at 9:00 and crafts at 10:00. The completed diagram looks like this:

	Sw	H	FP	N	C	R	So	B
9	X	X	O	X	X	X	X	X
10	X	X	X	X	O	X	X	X
11	?	?	X	X	X	X	X	X
12	X	X	X	X	X	X	X	X
1	X	X	X	O	X	X	X	X
2	X	X	X	X	X	X	O	X
3	X	X	X	X	X	O	X	X

Now, by checking the diagram against the answer choices, we can see that only (D) is correct.

5.   **(C)**   is the correct answer. Construct a diagram with the days of the week across the top and the initials of the applicants down the side. Starting with condition 2, we can place X's for the men in the boxes for Monday and Thursday, and we can place X's for the women in the boxes for Tuesday and Wednesday. Next, we can place O's under Monday for Abby, Clara, and Demi (condition 5), and we can place X's under the other days, since no one is interviewed more than once (condition 4). Betty cannot be interviewed on Thursday, so put an X for her under Thursday. Betty cannot be interviewed on Monday, since only three people can be interviewed on the same day, and Abby, Clara, and Demi are being interviewed on Monday. Betty must be interviewed on Friday, then. Place an O for her on Friday, and X's for her on the other days. By looking at the diagram we see that everyone but Edie has been eliminated on Thursday. Since at least one person must be interviewed each day, Edie is interviewed on Thursday. Place an O for her on Thursday, and place X's for her on the other days. Vic must be interviewed last (condition 8), so he must be interviewed after Betty on Friday. Place an O for him on Friday, and X's for him on the other days. Zeke must be interviewed before Edie and Betty (condition 3), which means he is interviewed on Tuesday or Wednesday. We can put an X in Friday for Zeke, and question marks on Tuesday and Wednesday. Yosef and Wade must be interviewed on the same day (condition 9). They cannot be interviewed on Friday, since Betty and Vic are interviewed that day, and no more than three can be interviewed on the same day. Put X's in Friday for Yosef and Wade. Yosef and Wade must be interviewed on Tuesday or Wednesday, so put question marks for them on those days. Even though we cannot tell whether Yosef, Wade, and Zeke are interviewed on Tuesday or Wednesday, we know that Yosef and Wade are interviewed on one of those days, while Zeke is interviewed on the other. If they were all interviewed on the same day, either Tuesday or Wednesday would have no interviews, which is not permitted. To show that Yosef and Wade must be interviewed on the same day, we will circle the question marks for them on Tuesday and Wednesday. Now by looking at the diagram we can see that (A) is false because Edie is interviewed on Thursday. (B) is not necessarily true, since Zeke can be interviewed on Tuesday or Wednesday. (C) must be true, because Wade and Yosef must be interviewed on the same day. If Zeke is also interviewed on that day, then either Tuesday or Wednesday would have no interviews. Neither (D) nor (E) is necessarily true, since Wade and Yosef can be interviewed on Tuesday if Zeke is interviewed on Wednesday; or they can be interviewed on Wednesday if Zeke is interviewed on Tuesday.

		M	T	W	Th	F
	A	O	X	X	X	X
	B	X	X	X	X	O
Women	C	O	X	X	X	X
	D	O	X	X	X	X
	E	X	X	X	O	X
	Z	X	?	?	X	X
Men	Y	X	?	?	X	X
	W	X	?	?	X	X
	V	X	X	X	X	O

TIPS FOR FOLLOWING DIRECTIONS

Keep this in mind:

➤ Tip 1   As you can see, you are asked to choose the response that most accurately and completely answers each questions. Although other answers may seem to be correct, only one is the best answer so make sure to work through the problem carefully.

➤ Tip 2   You are also instructed that drawing diagrams may be useful, so use them whenever possible.

TIPS FOR ANSWERING QUESTIONS

Consider these tips:

➤ Tip 1   Do not spend too much time on any one question; pace yourself.

➤ Tip 2   Do not rush to finish every problem in the section.

➤ Tip 3   Read the problems carefully; make no assumptions.

➤ Tip 4   Family tree and ordering relationships are often the basis for the questions which appear in this section.

➤ Tip 5   When using charts, do not make them complicated.

➤ Tip 6   Since you are not required to have knowledge of the subject presented in a passage, all of the information you will need to answer a question correctly will be provided in the passage. Occasionally, a question will include additional information not found in the passage, but this information can only be used to answer that particular question.

CHAPTER 7

Analytical Reasoning Practice Test

ANALYTICAL REASONING
PRACTICE TEST

1. (A) (B) (C) (D) (E)
2. (A) (B) (C) (D) (E)
3. (A) (B) (C) (D) (E)
4. (A) (B) (C) (D) (E)
5. (A) (B) (C) (D) (E)
6. (A) (B) (C) (D) (E)
7. (A) (B) (C) (D) (E)
8. (A) (B) (C) (D) (E)
9. (A) (B) (C) (D) (E)
10. (A) (B) (C) (D) (E)
11. (A) (B) (C) (D) (E)
12. (A) (B) (C) (D) (E)
13. (A) (B) (C) (D) (E)
14. (A) (B) (C) (D) (E)
15. (A) (B) (C) (D) (E)
16. (A) (B) (C) (D) (E)
17. (A) (B) (C) (D) (E)
18. (A) (B) (C) (D) (E)
19. (A) (B) (C) (D) (E)
20. (A) (B) (C) (D) (E)
21. (A) (B) (C) (D) (E)
22. (A) (B) (C) (D) (E)
23. (A) (B) (C) (D) (E)
24. (A) (B) (C) (D) (E)
25. (A) (B) (C) (D) (E)
26. (A) (B) (C) (D) (E)
27. (A) (B) (C) (D) (E)
28. (A) (B) (C) (D) (E)
29. (A) (B) (C) (D) (E)
30. (A) (B) (C) (D) (E)

ANALYTICAL REASONING
PRACTICE TEST

DIRECTIONS: Each group of questions in this section is based on a set of conditions. In answering some of the questions, it may be useful to draw a rough diagram. Choose the response that most accurately and completely answers each question.

Questions 1 – 5 are based on the following.

The Bocce family has just hosted a 50th wedding anniversary party for Guido and Maria at their favorite Italian restaurant, Salducci's. Among the family members attending were the following:

Jim Jr., who is Maria's only greatgrandson, Kathy's grandson, and the only child of Jim, who is Kathy's only child

Maria's only two siblings: Dora and Tony

Jack, the oldest of Dora's two grandsons, and the only son of her daughter Jane

Carol, Jane's only sibling

Tony's only daughter, Louise, who has one daughter, named Mitzi

Guido and Maria's six daughters; Guido and Maria have no sons

Tony's grandnephew, Joe

Keep in mind that in this family

• children of first cousins are considered second cousins

• children of second cousins are considered third cousins

• a grandnephew is the grandson of one's brother or sister

• a greatgrandnephew is the greatgrandson of one's brother or sister

• neither Maria nor Guido has been married before

• five of Guido and Maria's daughters are childless

1.   Joe's closest blood relative is

(A)   Kathy.   (D)   Tony.

(B)   Jane.   (E)   Maria.

(C)   Carol.

2.   What relation is Jim Jr. to Tony?

(A)   Nephew   (D)   No blood relation

(B)   Grandnephew   (E)   Cousin

(C)   Greatgrandnephew

3.   Which of the following statements about Joe and Jack is false?

(A)   Joe and Jack are first cousins.

(B)   Joe and Jack are second cousins.

(C)   Joe and Jack are Dora's grandsons.

(D)   Joe and Jack are Maria's grandnephews.

(E)   Joe and Jack are Jim's second cousins.

4.   Louise's daughter, Mitzi, is what relation to Jim?

(A)   First cousin   (D)   Aunt

(B)   Second cousin   (E)   No blood relation

(C)   Niece

5.   Which of the following statements about Joe is false?

(A)   Joe is Jim's first cousin.

(B)   Joe is Jim's second cousin.

(C)   Joe is Jane's nephew.

(D)   Joe is Dora's grandson.

(E)   Joe is Maria's grandnephew.

Questions 6 – 9 are based on the following.

Mr. Elan always coordinated the color of his sport coat, tie, and trousers. He had four sport coats, six pairs of trousers, and seven ties. Each sport coat could be worn with two different pairs of trousers and each coat and trouser combination always allowed a choice of three different ties. He always selected his sport coat first.

6. How many different ways can Mr. Elan wear these three articles of clothing and still conform to his color combinations?

   (A) 9   (D) 12

   (B) 24   (E) 18

   (C) 72

7. When one of his sport coats is at the cleaners, how many *fewer* combinations of attire does he have?

   (A) 4   (D) 7

   (B) 5   (E) Cannot determine

   (C) 6

8. Mr. Elan spilled food on one of his ties and discarded it and also sent one of his sport coats to the cleaners. How many combinations of attire does he now have available?

   (A) 18   (D) 20

   (B) 12   (E) Cannot determine

   (C) 24

9. If Mr. Elan purchased another sport coat that also coordinated with three of his ties and two pairs of his trousers, how many additional combinations could he wear that would conform to his color requirements?

   (A) 6   (D) 18

   (B) 30   (E) Cannot determine

   (C) 24

Questions 10 – 14 are based on the following.

Alvin, Frank, George, Henry, Sam, and Irving planned a week-long fishing trip to Lake Carlisle. However, two days before they were to depart, they argued over what type of bait was best for catching trout. The argument became quite heated, and some of the men were so angry with the others that they decided they would not go if the others went.

If both Sam and Alvin went, then Irving went.

If Irving went, then George went.

If Frank went, then Sam also went.

Either Sam or Henry will go.

Alvin went.

George did not go.

10.   How many of these men went on the fishing trip?

(A)   1   (D)   4

(B)   2   (E)   5

(C)   3

11.   Which of the following statements is true?

(A)   Either Sam didn't go or Alvin did go.

(B)   Sam went, but Alvin did not.

(C)   Frank went, and Sam did not.

(D)   Both Irving and Sam went.

(E)   Sam went, and Frank did not.

12.   If George had changed his mind and had gone on the fishing trip, but all other conditions remained the same, which of the statements below would follow with certainty?

(A)   Alvin did not go.   (D)   Frank did not go.

(B)   Irving did not go.   (E)   None went.

(C)   Henry did not go.

13. Which of the following does NOT follow from George not going?

    (A) Irving did not go.   (D) Irving went.

    (B) Alvin went.   (E) Henry went.

    (C) Sam did not go.

14. If Alvin had changed his mind and had decided not to go, but all of the other conditions remained the same, which of the following statements would follow with certainty?

    (A) Irving went.   (D) Sam did not go.

    (B) Sam went.   (E) None went.

    (C) Irving did not go.

Questions 15 – 18 are based on the following.

The quality control department of a clothing manufacturer inspected all garments according to four types of flaws: (1) color, (2) fabric quality, (3) seams, and (4) size. Inspectors forwarded defective garments to a supervisor to make a final decision. Inspectors attached tags to garments indicating the type of flaw according to the following: Type 1 = Red; Type 2 = Blue; Type 3 = Green; Type 4 = Yellow. Mistakes in color were re-dyed; flaws in fabric went to a "seconds" outlet; faulty seams were sent to be re-sewn; errors in sizing were sent to a "re-tag office"; and some were too defective to salvage. The final decision that a garment could be salvaged was made by Supervisors A, B, and C. Supervisor A made the decision on color and fabric problems; Supervisor B made the decision on seam and size problems; and Supervisor C reviewed garments with three or more kinds of defects. Supervisor D reviewed the recommendations from A, B, and/ or C to make the final decision on all articles to be discarded rather than repaired.

15. When a garment has a color blemish that can be corrected, what color code will be attached and which of the following people will be responsible for detecting the flaw, and making a decision about the garment?

    (A) Red, Inspector, Supervisors A and D

    (B) Blue, Inspector, Supervisors A and B

(C)   Red, Inspector, Supervisor A

(D)   Blue, Inspector, Supervisor B

(E)   Red, Inspector, Supervisors B and D

16.   When a garment has inspector tags that are Red, Blue, and Green attached and may not be repairable, which of the following people will be responsible for making a decision about the garment?

(A)   Supervisors A, B, and D

(B)   Supervisors A, C, and D

(C)   Supervisors B, C, and D

(D)   Supervisors C and D

(E)   Supervisors A, B, C, and D

17.   When a garment has a repairable flaw in color and seams what colors will be attached and who will be involved in processing this garment?

(A)   Blue, Yellow, Supervisors A and B

(B)   Red, Green, Inspector, Supervisors A and B

(C)   Red, Yellow, Inspector, Supervisors C and D

(D)   Red, Green, Supervisors A and B

(E)   Red, Blue, Inspector, Supervisors A, B, and C

18.   When a garment has the maximum number of flaws and cannot be repaired, how many people will be involved in the inspection and final decision about this garment?

(A)   1   (D)   4

(B)   2   (E)   5

(C)   3

Questions 19 – 23 are based on the following.

The Weymouth Ferry was fully loaded except for space for six tons of deck cargo. The purser had 10 crates that had not yet been brought aboard.

One crate weighed 1,000 pounds.

Two crates weighed a ton each.

Three crates each weighed a ton and a half.

The last four crates each weighed two tons.

19. What is the maximum number of these crates that can be stowed in the space available for deck cargo?

(A) 3   (D) 6

(B) 4   (E) 7

(C) 5

20. What is the minimum number of crates that can be taken aboard and exactly fill the available deck cargo space?

(A) 2   (D) 5

(B) 3   (E) 6

(C) 4

21. If the three ton-and-a-half crates are taken aboard, what is the maximum number of additional crates that can be stowed in the available space?

(A) 5   (D) 2

(B) 4   (E) 1

(C) 3

22. If the 1,000-pound crate costs $10 to ship, each one-ton crate costs $20, each ton-and-a-half crate costs $30 and each two-ton crate $25, what is the maximum shipping charge the purser can collect from the available tonnage?

(A) $75

(B) $90

(C) $110

(D) $120

(E) $150

23. If the 1,000-pound crate cost $10 to ship, each one ton crate costs $20, each ton-and-a-half crate costs $30 and each two-ton crate $25, how much shipping charge is the purser guaranteed if he uses at least half the available tonnage?

(A) $40

(B) $45

(C) $50

(D) $55

(E) $60

Questions 24 – 27 are based on the following.

The ACME company devised a code to retrieve files from their computer. Their access codes are limited to a total of eight letters or numbers (excluding 0). The letters must appear in alphabetical order and the numbers must appear in descending order. The letters cannot be adjacent to one another but the numbers can be. The code may begin with either a letter or a number but must end with a letter. At least three numbers and three letters must appear in each code.

24. Which of the following conforms to the requirements for the code?

(A) 8 B 6 H 4 M 2 L

(B) A 7 B 6 4 3 2 F

(C) B K 9 8 M O R 7

(D) 8 7 5 L 3 O 1 K

(E) R U N 4 I T N W

25. Which of the following first three parts of the code could meet the requirements of the code?

(A) A 7 B.....

(D) 7 A B.....

(B) A B 7.....

(E) X Y 4.....

(C) A 2 B.....

26. Which of the following last three parts of the code could meet the requirements of the code?

(A) .....A 7 M

(D) .....C 6 D

(B) .....C D 8

(E) .....8 E F

(C) .....A 2 D

27. Which of the following does *not* conform to the requirements for the code?

(A) B 8 G 6 4 K 2 X

(D) G 9 J 7 M 5 3 S

(B) 5 C 4 G 3 M 2 P

(E) A 4 B 3 C 2 D 1

(C) F H 7 J 6 K 4 I.

Questions 28 – 30 are based on the following.

A police lineup contained four men, one of whom was a thief. The lineup is graduated by height, with the tallest man on the left and the shortest on the right (from the witness's viewpoint). There are two men between Carl and Scott. Ricky is to the left of Bryan. The thief is third from the left. Scott is to the right of the thief.

28. Who is the thief?

(A) Scott

(D) Carl

(B) Bryan

(E) Cannot be determined

(C) Ricky

29. Who is the tallest?

    (A) Scott

    (B) Bryan

    (C) Ricky

    (D) Carl

    (E) Cannot be determined

30. Which of the following statements would, if added to the first six, be inconsistent with one or more of them?

    I.   The man on the far right is taller than Bryan.

    II. The witness named Scott as the thief.

    III. Ricky is between Carl and Bryan.

    (A) I only

    (B) I and II only

    (C) II and III only

    (D) II only

    (E) I, II, and III

ANALYTICAL REASONING
PRACTICE TEST

ANSWER KEY

1. (C)	7. (C)	13. (D)	19. (C)	25. (A)
2. (C)	8. (E)	14. (C)	20. (B)	26. (D)
3. (B)	9. (A)	15. (C)	21. (D)	27. (C)
4. (B)	10. (B)	16. (D)	22. (D)	28. (B)
5. (A)	11. (A)	17. (B)	23. (B)	29. (D)
6. (B)	12. (E)	18. (C)	24. (B)	30. (A)

Analytical Reasoning Detailed Explanations of Answers

Questions 1 – 5

Since each of the questions for this passage requires us to identify relationships between family members, we will first construct a family tree by going through the conditions and then we will turn to the questions.

We know that Guido and Maria have six daughters and no sons. We also know that five of their six daughters are childless, and that Jim Jr. is Maria's only greatgrandson, Kathy's grandson, and the only child of Jim, who is Kathy's only child.

From these conditions we can conclude that Kathy is Maria's daughter. The relationships expressed in these conditions may now be visually represented as follows:

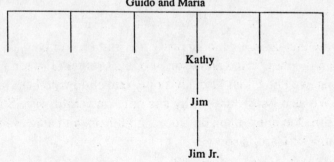

Since the remainder of the conditions focus on Maria and her two siblings Tony and Dora, the diagram below will focus on these three individuals.

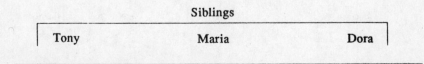

We also know from the conditions given that Dora (Maria's sister) has two children: Carol and Jane. It is also stated in the conditions that Jane has one son: Jack.

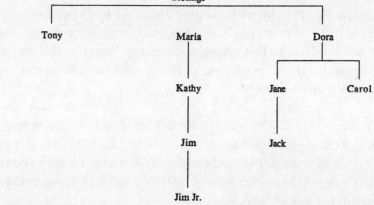

Going to Maria's brother Tony, we know that Louise is his only daughter and that she has one child. We know that the child is a female named Mitzi.

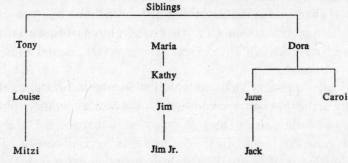

Finally, we know that Tony's grandnephew Joe is at the anniversary party. We know that a grandnephew is the grandson of one's brother or sister. Going back to the conditions, we know that Maria has only one child who has children, and that is Kathy. We also know that Kathy has only one child, Jim. So Joe is not Maria's grandson. Joe must, then, be Dora's grandson, and since Jane has only one son, Joe must be Carol's son.

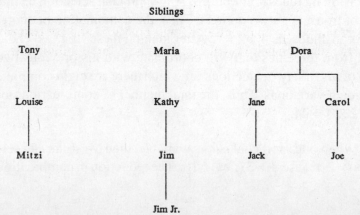

The diagram is now complete, and we can answer the questions.

1.   **(C)**   Question 1 asks us who Joe's closest blood relative is. Of the choices given, we can easily see that the correct answer is (C) Carol, who is his mother.

2.   **(C)**   Question 2 asks us what relation Jim Jr. is to Tony. Looking at the diagram, we see that Kathy is Tony's niece, her son Jim is Tony's grandnephew, and so Jim's son Jim Jr. is Tony's greatgrandnephew. Note that this corresponds to how "greatgrandnephew" is defined in the conditions. The correct answer, then, is (C) Greatgrandnephew.

3.   **(B)**   Question 3 asks which of the statements given about Joe and Jack is false. Looking at the diagram, we can see that Joe and Jack ARE first cousins. It follows, then, that they are not second cousins. It is not necessary to go through the remaining choices. The correct answer is (B) Joe and Jack are second cousins. This is the statement that is false.

4.   **(B)**   Question 4 asks us what relation Louise's daughter Mitzi is to Jim. Looking at the chart and at the definition of "second cousin," you can see that Mitzi and Jim are second cousins, i.e., they are children of first cousins (Louise and Kathy are first cousins). The correct answer is (B) Second cousin.

5.   **(A)**   Finally, question 5 asks us which of the given statements about Joe is false. Looking at the diagram, we know that Joe is Maria's grandnephew, that is, the grandson of Maria's sister Dora. We also know that Joe is Dora's grandson and Jane's nephew. And again, by the definition of "second cousin," Joe is Jim's second cousin (that is, they are the children of first cousins Carol and Kathy). However, Joe is NOT Jim's first cousin. The correct answer to question 5, then, is (A) Joe is Jim's first cousin, that is, it is false that Joe is Jim's second cousin.

6.   **(B)**   Mr. Elan has three decisions to make. Each decision becomes dependent on his previous choice. He can first select any one of four sport coats, thus his first decision includes four options. Any sport coat selection he makes limits his choice of trousers to two options. Thus, the combination of sport coats and trousers he can choose is $4 \times 2 = 8$. After making these first two choices he can then select from three ties that will coordinate with his previous two choices. Thus, each of his first two selections (of which there are eight combinations) has three additional variations. Thus, the total number of combinations available to him is $4 \times 2 \times 3 = 24$.

7.   **(C)**   When one sport coat is not available, then Mr. Elan can select from 3 (sport coats) $\times$ 2 (trousers) $\times$ 3 (ties) = 18. The reduction in combinations of attire

is 24 – 18 = 6. The answer could also be calculated by determining the number of combinations provided by one sport coat; 1 × 2 × 3 = 6.

8.   **(E)**   No information was provided about the damaged tie to indicate if it coordinated with one or more of the coats remaining in Mr. Elan's closet.

9.   **(A)**   Adding another sport coat would provide him with a choice of 5 (sport coats) × 2 (trousers) × 3 (ties) = 30. He would add 30 – 24 = 6 new combinations to his wardrobe. Or, you can multiply 1 (sport coat) × 2 (trousers) × 3 (ties) = 6 to determine the result of adding one sport coat to the wardrobe.

10.   **(B)**   Following the suggested method, we will group together conditions that have terms in common.

First, conditions 2 and 6 are grouped together.
(2) If Irving went, then George went.
(6) George did not go.
We can conclude that (conclusion 1) Irving did not go.

Now we pair this conclusion with condition 1.
(1) If both Sam and Alvin went, then Irving went.
(Conclusion 1) Irving did not go.

We can conclude that (conclusion 2):
Both Sam and Alvin did not go, that is, either Sam did not go or Alvin did not go.

Now we pair this conclusion with condition 5.
(Conclusion 2) Either Sam did not go or Alvin did not go.
(5) Alvin went.
We can conclude that (conclusion 3) Sam did not go.

Now we pair up condition 3 with conclusion 3.
(3) If Frank went, then Sam also went.
(Conclusion 3) Sam did not go.
We can conclude that (conclusion 4) Frank did not go.

Finally, we pair condition 4 with conclusion 3.
(4) Either Sam or Henry will go.
(Conclusion 3) Sam did not go.
We can conclude that (conclusion 5) Henry went.

In sum, we know that Alvin and Henry went, but that George, Irving, Sam, and Frank did not go. The correct answer to question 10, then, is (B) 2.

11. **(A)** Question 11 gives us five statements, and we have to determine which of the five statements is true. Having already deduced conclusions from the conditions, this question is easily answered. We know that Sam did not go on the fishing trip, so (B), (D), and (E) are false. We also know that Frank did not go, so (C) is false. The only option left is (A). It is true that Sam did not go, and it is also true that Alvin did go. The correct answer, then, is (A) Either Sam didn't go or Alvin did go.

12. **(E)** Question 12 changes one of the original conditions, and you have to determine what follows from the new condition "George did go on the fishing trip" and the remaining original conditions.

None of the conditions states that George will go only if Irving goes, so we can't conclude anything about Irving. Also, since the conditions don't tell us that Irving will go only if both Sam and Alvin go, we can't conclude anything about Sam and Alvin. Finally, as Frank and Sam are linked together in one condition, and Sam and Henry in another, and since we can't conclude anything about Sam, we can't conclude anything about Frank or Henry. The correct answer, then is (E) None went.

13. **(D)** Question 13 asks us which of the options does NOT follow from George not going. Again, we can refer to the conclusions that we have already deduced in question 10. We know Irving definitely did not go, Henry and Alvin did, and Sam did not. The correct answer, then, is (D) Irving went. That is, it does not follow that Irving went.

14. **(C)** This question also changes a condition. Here, the condition "Alvin went" is changed to "Alvin did not go." However, all of the other conditions remain the same, and you are asked to determine which of the statements presented follow with certainty from this changed condition in conjunction with the remaining original conditions. In answering this question, we must again group the conditions together.

First, we will group conditions 2 and 6 together.
(2) If Irving went, then George went.
(6) George did not go.
We can conclude that (conclusion 1) Irving did not go.

Now we can group condition 1 with conclusion 1.
    (1) If both Sam and Alvin went, then Irving went.
    (Conclusion 1) Irving did not go.

We can conclude that it is not true that both Sam and Alvin went, that is, either Sam did not go or Alvin did not go. We know from the changed condition that Alvin did not go. However, it could be true that Sam did not go either. In other words, even though we know that Alvin did not go, it does not follow with certainty that Sam did go or that he did not. So we cannot conclude anything about Sam. However, looking at our options, we see that one corresponds to a conclusion we have already deductively drawn, and that is "Irving did not go." The correct answer, then, is (C) Irving did not go.

15. **(C)** See number 18.

16. **(D)** See number 18.

17. **(B)** See number 18.

18. **(C)** It is important to identify the three stations which garments might pass through during the inspection process. Station 1 is staffed by inspectors who tag defective garments, station 2 is staffed by Supervisors A, B, and C who make salvage decisions, and Supervisor D who is the only one authorized to discard garments. After this understanding is clear, then you can recognize which garments may pass through one station (the inspector) if it is not defective, a second station (the supervisor) if it is defective but is not to be discarded, and a third station (Supervisor D) for a decision about discarding. The color coding will help you decide the routing of defective garments.

19. **(C)** To get the largest number in, begin with the smallest and build up until capacity is reached. The total capacity is six tons or 12,000 pounds. So, one crate weighing 1,000 pounds can go in, giving a total of 1,000 pounds. Look at totals after various additions (in 1,000 pound units).

total crates	#/weight	weight	total weight
1	1 @ 1	1	1
3	2 @ 2	4	5
6	3 @ 3	9	14

This is too much, but not putting all of the last group in gives

| 5 | 2 @ 3 | 6 | 11 |

So, a total of five crates can be stowed, answer (C). Clearly, using any of the heavier crates will allow no more crates to be stowed. Using only one of the 3,000 pound crates and one of the 4,000 pounders would still permit only five crates, though it would bring the total weight up to 12,000 pounds.

As for the other answers, the chart above shows a way to have only three crates aboard and still have room for more (1 @ 1 and 2 @ 2 leaves room for 2 @ 3), so (A) is wrong. Similarly, (B) is shown wrong by the possibility of having four crates consisting of 1 @ 1, 2 @ 2, 1 @ 3 and still having room for 1 @ 3 or even 1 @ 4. (D) fails because the lightest possible combinations using six crates is the combination listed first above and that weighs more than is available. Finally, (E) fails since it must inevitably weigh even more than a combination of six crates and that is already more than allowed.

20. **(B)**   To find the minimum number, start with the heaviest, in this case, the 4,000-pound crates. Three of them will exactly fill the 12,000 pound limit, so answer (B) is correct. Using lighter crates will require more crates to come up to the required weight. (A) has to be wrong, for the most that two crates could weigh is 8,000 pounds (2 @ 4,000) which is less than the amount allowed. The remaining cases fail because five is the maximum number of crates that can be stowed.

21. **(D)**   Given that 3 @ 3,000, i.e., 9,000 pounds, are stowed, only 3,000 pounds remain. With the crates available, the maximum number to fill that space would be

| 1 @ 1 | 1 | 1 |
| 1 @ 2 | 2 | 3 |

So, two more crates could be gotten on. The fact that this is possible means that (E), only one more crate, does not represent the maximum. On the other hand, any combination involving more crates will weigh more than the permitted amount. (A), (B), and (C) must, then, all be wrong. In addition, each of these would involve more than five crates being stowed (the 3 @ 3 plus the addition number > 2) and five is the maximum number of crates which could be stowed.

22. **(D)**   Except for the two-ton crates, all the crates cost $10 per 1,000 pounds to ship. The two-ton crates cost less per 1,000 pounds. So, the maximum shipping charge would come from shipping 12,000 pounds at the higher rate, i.e., $120 total, answer (D). The purser could reach full capacity at this rate in several ways, for example, one 1,000-pound crate, one 2,000-pound crate, and three 3,000-pound crates. (A) gives the rate for full capacity at the lower rate, three two-ton crates @ $25. But the higher rate is available and gives a larger total charge. (B) could be reached by using two two-ton crates and two one-ton ones, but still uses part of the lower rate and so does not maximize the total charge. (C) is probably the result of not putting on a full six tons of cargo, using perhaps one 1,000-pound crate, two one-ton crates, and two one-and-a-half-ton crates — the maximum number but not the maximum tonnage allowable, and so not as high a charge as possible. (E) is not a possible charge at all, since even at the higher rate, it would require 15,000 pounds of cargo and there is only 12,000 available.

23. **(B)**   The guaranteed total would be the minimum obtainable under the condition, that he use at least 6,000 pounds. Since, except for the cheaper two-ton crates, crates go for $10 per 1,000 pounds. This total must be at most $60, i.e., all 6,000 pounds at the highest rate. But it is possible to take some of this tonnage in two-ton crates at the lower rate, so $60 is not the minimum under the conditions and (E) is wrong. In particular, the purser could load one two-ton crate at $25 and one one-ton crate at $20 for a total of $45 dollars in charges for three tons. So, (C) and (D) are also not minimum charges. On the other hand, there is no way to get down to $40 without taking on less than three tons, for, at the higher rate, $40 would only pay for two tons of freight, while the lower rate only applies to units of two tons each, one of which would be $25 but too light and two of which would be $50 and also too heavy. The nearest combinations of rates would be a two-ton crate and a 1,000-pound crate, which would be only $35 and would be too light or the two-ton and the one-ton which give the actual minimum noted. So, (A) does not give a minimum for the given conditions.

24. **(B)**   See number 27.

25. **(A)**   See number 27.

26. **(D)**   See number 27.

27. **(C)**   The answers in this series require attention to the conditions stipulated in the passage. The best way to answer each question is to examine each option and look for a violation of one or more of the following requirements:

1. Alphabetical order of letters

2. Descending order of numbers

3. Letters cannot be adjacent to each other

4. Code must end with letter

5. At least three letters and numbers in each code

6. Code must start or end with letters or numbers that conform to the requirements. In question 25 choice (C) is wrong because the number 2 is the first number in the sequence and it would not be possible to include three digits in descending order unless the first number was 3 or higher.

28. **(B)** Since there are only four men, and Carl and Scott are on the outside, and Ricky is to the left of Bryan, the order must be (from left to right) Carl, Ricky, Bryan, Scott. The man third from the left is Bryan; therefore, Bryan is the thief.

29. **(D)** The tallest man is on the left. Since there are only four men, and two of them are between Carl and Scott, Carl and Scott must be on the outside. Since Scott is to the right of the thief, he cannot be on the left side of the line and therefore Carl must be the tallest.

30. **(A)** Statement I would be inconsistent with the premise that states that heights shall be in descending order from left to right. Statement II does not contradict any of the given statements; the fact that a witness identified Scott as the thief is not inconsistent with the fact that Bryan is the thief. Statement III is perfectly consistent, and may in fact be deduced from the given premises.

Available at your local bookstore or order directly from us by sending in coupon below.

Available at your local bookstore or order directly from us by sending in coupon below.

REA's Test Preps
The Best in Test Preparation

The REA "Test Preps" are far more comprehensive than any other test series. They contain more tests with much more extensive explanations than others on the market. Each book provides several complete practice exams, based on the most recent tests given in the particular field. Every type of question likely to be given on the exams is included. Each individual test is followed by a complete answer key. **The answers are accompanied by full and detailed explanations.** By studying each test and the explanations which follow, students will become well-prepared for the actual exam.

REA has published over 40 Test Preparation volumes in several series. They include: